Angelic Energies

By

Sean Bradley
(The Barefoot Angel Man)

PublishAmerica
Baltimore

First printing

Front Cover Picture: *The Archangel Metatron* painted by Alison Knox of *EveryDay Angels*, UK

ISBN: 1-4137-4697-7
PUBLISHED BY PUBLISHAMERICA, LLLP
www.publishamerica.com
Baltimore

Printed in the United States of America

Message to Sean Jude Bradley
17 March 2003

"Given to Sean Jude Bradley—heal souls broken by man in ignorance and pain."

The Archangel Metatron
painted by Alison Knox of *EveryDay Angels*, UK

Foreword

Do you believe in Angels? Or is it more than that? Maybe it is that feeling, that knowing, that is beyond belief. I have always felt the presence and support of something in my life that has guided me, but for many years may not have identified that loving presence as Angelic Energy.

Many things have happened in my life that have drawn me closer to working with the Angels and recognising the gifts that they constantly bring to each and every one of us.

The past seven years have been a life changing experience for me. It began when my husband and I decided to try and save the derelict St. Francis Church and Friary in Gorton, Manchester. With cherished memories of happy schooldays and as an altar boy, Gorton Monastery had played a significant role in my husband's formative years. I visited this magnificent ruin in 1996 and was overwhelmed by the energy of the place. At the time I had no idea of the size and commitment of the work we were about to undertake or the challenges of the journey ahead.

All of those experiences could fill a book of their own, and may do so one day.

We realise that our work has only just begun. We have learnt that the project is no longer about saving a building, but much more about working with the unique energies of a very powerful sacred site and allowing that love to inspire and heal a much wider community. Along the way we have been joined by many like-minded souls who I'm sure have been sent to us by the Angels when the timing was right and their skills were needed the most.

One of those special people was Sean Bradley who was introduced to me when he came to do an Angels Workshop in Gorton several years ago. Sean is a gifted and inspirational teacher who, through his gentle and humorous style, creates a unique healing atmosphere for his audience. The Angels brought love, joy and laughter to Gorton that day and I felt privileged to be in their company.

A year or so later Sean offered to spend a day with our small and exhausted hard working team who at the time were still struggling to raise the much-needed funds for the Monastery. It was a memorable day for us all, which refreshed and relaxed us. At the same time it was like being bathed in love and light, an uplifting experience that recharged our depleted batteries and reassured us that our work was important and we were on the right path. It is such a privilege for us to have been given custody of such an important project and sometimes it is overwhelming. We all feel that it would never have got this far without the support and guidance from the Angelic Realms.

Ironically, the only things that remain and haven't been vandalised in the former church of St. Francis are the beautiful carved angels looking down on us from on high. I'm sure they are there as a reminder of the loving, divine guidance that helps us through each day. So it may not surprise you to know that we have named our site 'The Angels, Manchester' in acknowledgement and thanks for the Angelic Energies that continue to surround us.

If we were all able to embrace the Angelic Energies daily and let it guide our lives what a different place this world could be. It is a delight and honour to know Sean Bradley as he brings a host of loving Angels ever closer to many people's lives. This book is a demonstration of his work.

Enjoy this book and the many Angel blessings it will bring you.

Elaine Griffiths
Project Director & Co-Founder
The Monastery of St. Francis & Gorton Trust & The
Angels, Manchester

May 2004

This book is dedicated to Rob, my Anam Cara, my soul mate. He heard my cry in the wilderness and provided sanctuary. I am eternally grateful for his love, guidance and support.

Acknowledgements

There are so many people I wish to thank for being there for me during this time of soul searching. It has been testing time. There has been laughter and there have been tears as I have shed the old to discover and claim the new. If there is anyone I have forgotten to mention, may they please rest assured that I am deeply grateful for their kindness and support.

Firstly a special thank you to Evelynn Hannah for her help with the editing and the typing of this book. I thank her for her time and patience. Her wisdom and intuition have been invaluable.

I send my love and gratitude to my parents, Anna and Jack, my sisters Eileen and Angela and the many other family members to numerous to mention. Dr Shakleton, Maria, Lorraine, Sandra my Reiki Master, Siobhan and Phil, Stuart Van Bellen and his beloved family. I would also like to thank Ramo Kabbani who founded the Prozac Survivor's Group in the UK. Sister Agatha and all at Ty Mam Duw.

Thanks to Alison Knox of Everyday Angels for her inspired angel paintings and for her friendship and support. Alison painted the picture on the cover of this book

To my dear friend Hazel Hunt who painted the pictures of the Robin and the trees, which have been used throughout the book, and to all those who contributed poems and testimonials I say thank you.

To Martin, Helen, Geoff, Di Granger and all my students,

both here in the UK and in Ireland. A special thank you to all the clients I have worked with. Their honest feedback and constructive criticism have been invaluable.

A big thank you to Jimmy France of Luk Luk Productions and Jeremy Parr of Sound Designers for their for providing the music for the meditation CDs.

A big thank you to all my colleagues in Manchester and North Wales. To Ellen and Ann who gave so much and asked for very little in return.

A big thank you to one of my student therapists Janet Quigley for the poem "Dedication to Sean 'The Barefoot Angel Man'".

Last but not least, my two best pals Ellie and Shimola our West Highland Terriers. They are healers and light workers in their own right and their love has always been both selfless and unconditional.

In Loving Memory

Of my beloved friend Brother Eddie. He gave unstintingly to all who knew him and to many who didn't. His love, wisdom, and ready laughter are sincerely and deeply missed.

Introduction

I was born in Glasgow on the 21st of December 1948 and there I stayed till I was a year old when my parents took me to live in Dublin. I consider myself a true Brit as I have lived, at one time or another, in Scotland, Wales, Ireland, and now England.

I had a normal childhood in Dublin. I was brought up Catholic and was educated by the famous Irish Christian Brothers. At the age of sixteen, I entered the novitiate house of studies of the Alexian Order in Cobh, Co. Cork. Three years later I became a professed monk and took vows of poverty, celibacy, and obedience. I served in monasteries in Northern Ireland, London, Manchester and Chicago in the U.S.A. I remained with the order for eight years when, after much soul searching, I made the decision to leave monastic life.

I continued with my nursing studies and eventually qualified as a State Registered Nurse. I was very excited and keen to introduce some alternative therapies into my work with the terminally ill, even then I felt that patients could benefit enormously from some of these practises. During the 1980s I became attuned to Reiki levels 1, 2, and 3 and completed a Diploma Course in Pastoral Counselling. Over the next few years I went on to achieve a Certificate in Business Studies, a Diploma in Garden Design from the Open University and a two year course in Horticulture at Manchester University. All these things added an exciting new dimension to my healing work.

When I was 46 my life changed completely. I had been working long hours for many years and was on the verge of burnout, I was physically and emotionally exhausted. Then my best friend Eddie died of cancer. His death had a profound effect on me, it was the final straw, I could no longer cope and so I sought help from my Doctor. He advised me to take Prozac. I did, and due to its affects, over the next year I lost everything. I lost my home, my partner of twenty years, my job, my liberty, and my self-respect.

It was a time of great uncertainty in my life and I prayed for help and guidance. The answer came in the form of two lovely 'light workers' called Maria and Lorraine who introduced me to a completely different side of the Angelic Realms. (Up till this point my view of angels had been very much coloured by my life in the Catholic Church). Through them I 'met' the Archangel Metatron, the guy with the thirty-six pairs of wings. I was completely in awe of the magnitude of his energy, and, so began a deep and lasting love affair with the angelic realms.

I was now beginning to sense the presence of angels and to know of their love for me. I was encouraged to take back control of my life. So, against the advice of my GP, I went over to Dublin and spent the next couple of months being weaned off the Prozac. On the 29th September 2001 I went self-employed and invested what little savings I had in working for the angelic realm.

Around this time I met Evelynn. She also works with angelic energies doing healing and soul growth readings. She encouraged me to look at my past from a different point of view and try to see the positive. I am very happy to say that I can now look back on those very difficult times and see them for what they are, learning experiences. I can now remember those times without feeling the emotional pain that they used to cause me.

I now live, very happily, in Cumbria with my partner Rob and our two West Highland Terriers, Miss Ellie and Shimola. My aim in writing this book is to bring the unconditional love and healing of the angelic realms to those who have not yet discovered it for themselves. Therapeutic Touch and Angel Energies have been invaluable to me in my journey through those difficult experiences. I hope you will find it as beneficial as I have.

Love and light,
Sean

To read Sean's story in full see his forthcoming book *Through Trauma We are Reborn–The Sean Bradley Story*.

I believe that where there is life there is hope.
Where there is hope, there is love
And where there is love, there God is!

-Sean Bradley

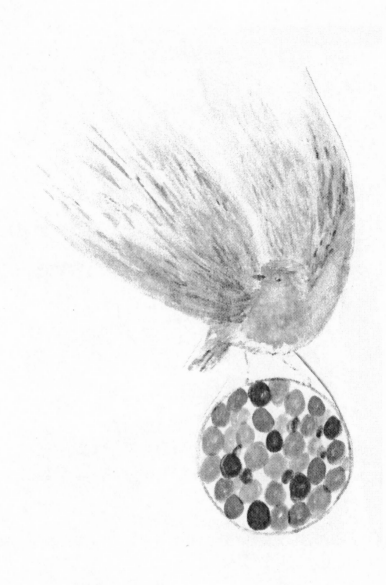

THERAPEUTIC TOUCH

Channelling Divine Love
Through Therapeutic Touch

Writing this book has been one of, if not, the biggest challenge of my entire life. The actual process of writing about 'Therapeutic Channelling and Touch' has made me look back and seek answers to the many unanswered questions about my life. These questions were on a variety of subjects such as my belief systems, negative thought patterns, victim-ness, the Catholic Church and its teachings on sexuality, spirituality and healing therapies. Before I explain my understanding of what Therapeutic Channelling is all about and why it is so effective as a healing form, I feel it is worth mentioning where I came from and how it touched my life.

As a committed Christian for many years, I tried to live out the simple message laid down by my role model Jesus Christ the barefoot Galilean, the Jewish carpenter from Nazareth. I tried to follow Christ's teachings, but I now realise that I was not really living out his message of simplicity and love. Somewhere in the maze of my life's experiences I lost that childlike simplicity and became fearful not fearless. Throughout my years of working as a nursing monk attached to a religious order, it is ironic that I never knew the joy of being in God's service. There was a deep-rooted fear inside me that prevented me from seeing the light of God and feeling the healing touch of his Divine love upon my soul.

I now accept that my spirituality was hindered by negative

beliefs and thought patterns that had stopped my simple faith from being expressed. The years spent living with these negative thoughts and beliefs had a destructive effect on my spiritual growth. It felt like a slow and lingering death. I felt as if I could not do anything right, religion not spirit was in control of my life. The first time I experienced the power of divine love through healing touch I realised I needed to take back control of my life. After many years in the shadows, I realised that I was living a self-imposed exile because I had relinquished my personal power.

Without wishing to apportion any blame I realised that my feelings and beliefs about God were influenced not by love but by fear. I was brought up in a society where life was greatly influenced by the Catholic Church. I feel that the preaching of hell and damnation has enabled the Church to retain power over its people for years. Whilst I believe in God I believe that the bible has been influenced by man and edited over the years. How much of it is now misinterpreted and misrepresented? I do not know, but I believe in God's love and his total acceptance of all of us. I feel that religion for me was being afraid of Hell and spirituality was something I came to after going through my own personal hell.

In retrospect I feel that from an early age I was steered towards the negative values of self-hate, self-condemnation, poor self-image and very low self-esteem. Like so many of my peers I went with the flow of the tide of negativism which ultimately affected my life, my creativity and my ability to see and accept that I was loved and accepted by God.

Throughout my life's journey I accepted the 'truths' of my faith wholly and without question. Before my introduction to channelled healing in 2001, I would never have dreamed of challenging the Church or any of its teachings. Now from an open heart and with integrity I often make challenges to the Divine and to the angelic realms and I do so in love.

Working with this therapy the God I see is one of absolute joy, liberation, and love. Through channelling divine love into my soul on a daily basis I have experienced pure healing from Source. (The Creator). I have seen the face of God. It is like a shining star in the heavens, radiating unconditional love into my being. My mind, body, and soul are infused with joy and the total acceptance that I am a child of God, a co-creator with the Divine—for the Divine. Through Therapeutic Channelling, the Divine touches each and every one of us and allows us to reclaim our dignity, self-worth and respect.

I visit Ireland fairly regularly to visit family and to do workshops. Most of my clients there grew up in similar circumstance to myself. At the last workshop I did there a large proportion of the forty participants said that they felt they had been directly or indirectly abused by the church. They said that they felt as though they had been 'stripped of their Divinity.' I was deeply saddened by this but, because of the years I had spent as a monk in the Alexian Order, I could understand what they meant. Towards the end of that very powerful day, three beautiful women approached me to say thank you for understanding their pain. They were former nuns who had given the Church the best years of their lives and were deeply wounded souls searching for a purpose to their time on this planet.

After the workshop, I invited the women to join me and spend a short time in quiet prayer and asked for them to be supported and empowered to continue their healing process. Afterwards we shared a 'group' hug and went our separate ways. A few months later I found out that the healing received that day and the tears that were shed were instrumental in them being able to move forward.

I believe that Therapeutic Touch has been in existence since the beginning of time. I have no evidence to support this view, but I sense that it had its roots in ancient civilizations. The most famous user of therapeutic touch was Jesus and Mary in turn touched him as she anointed his feet before his crucifixion.

*Light can increase your vibration, amplify the
Strength of your positive thoughts, and open your
Heart. You can link with it, harness its power, and
Create good all around you.*

-Elizabeth Kubler-Ross

Ellie and Shimola

Thinging Back—
Clues and Favourite Memories

There were many times when I was a young boy that the local children would bring their sick pets for me to make well. I would say a prayer asking God and St Francis to heal them. Word soon got round and eventually my Granny had a word with me and asked me to stop turning her beautiful front garden into a hospital for sick animals. She was not too pleased but she was eventually won over and I have very fond memories of her helping me to make bandages out of old sheets. They were days of an innocent and childlike trust in God. My understanding of healing was somewhat childlike and it remains so to this day. Along the way some people have challenged my naivety and simplicity. I have always seen it as a strength rather that a weakness.

I recall an incident that occurred when I was five years old. My father was tidying up broken glass from the greenhouse and I being curious decided to go and investigate. I fell into the broken glass. I still have the 'v' shaped scar on my leg. There was blood everywhere and my mum ran down the road to get my Granny. I believed that Granny had miraculous powers from God and I knew she would stop the pain and bleeding and make everything alright. She washed my leg and kissed it and I felt better instantly. It left a lasting impression on me. My destiny was set and some years later I went into healing work as a nursing monk.

In my childlike trust I believe that where there is love

there is light and where there is light there is love. I believe that when we open our minds and ask God for help the help is given. I believe that the healing process begins as soon as we set our intention and desire to change.

In the late seventies and early eighties the nursing journals carried several articles on Therapeutic Touch and how nurses could enroll in specialist courses run by an American nurse called Kruger Kunz. It was a good course, which we all found beneficial but we all agreed that we had been using the energy already but had not given it a name. When I look back, I can see that channelling this energy was part of my daily routine. It was not a conscious thing the energy had been flowing through me long before I realised it was there. The therapy that I offer to clients is not something that I invented it is a gift from God, another tool in the healing toolbox to use to help both others and myself. My hope is to empower them to heal themselves. I have many wonderful memories of the benefits of this healing which I have been privileged to administer.

On one occasion a good friend called round to see me, and after a few minutes I could tell from her body language that she was in a lot of discomfort. I gently held her hands and asked the angels to surround her with love. Then I invited Jesus to come and touch the areas that were causing her pain. There was no formal ritual or procedure; my actions were instinctive as I opened myself up to offer healing to this courageous soul.

In early 2003 I was booked to go and do an Angel Healing Day in a very nice hotel in Dublin. I was assured that it would be well attended and that I would more than cover my expenses. When I arrived at the conference room there were only two people waiting for me. My two sisters Eileen and Angela made the number up to four. The number four is significant is it the number of angel miracles. Miracles certainly happened for me that day.

One of the participants, Kathleen told us of the years of child abuse she had suffered at the hands of her father. We were all very moved by her story and humbled by her openness. After we had done the healing process and meditation she shared that she had felt angels touch her and that she realised that she would have to deal with the abuse issue before she could move on. It was a good day, which all five of us enjoyed.

Later that night back at my sister Angela's house I was giving myself a hard time because of the low turn out. I was also concerned because I had not made nearly enough money to even cover my expenses. I was doubting myself and questioning whether I should give up healing. My sister Eileen reassured me that the feedback from the day and all the previous workshops in Ireland was very positive and that I should keep going with the healing work.

On my return to the UK, I told the story to my dear friend Sister Agatha. She informed me "If I only touch one soul for God, then I had done the work of the Master." Those words have stayed with me ever since and I trust that all is as it should be regardless of the number of people in the room.

I met Kathleen again about four weeks later and she told me the rest of her story. The man who had abused her for all those years was actually her uncle and not her father. She discovered that her biological father was dying of cancer. He lived some distance away, but she felt she needed to go and make her peace, which she did. She said that the pure love she had received from the angels had empowered her to deal with it and then let it go. She hugged me and we shed many tears together.

In the summer of 2003 I was up a ten-foot ladder painting the outside of the house. I heard a 'thud' below me. When I looked down I could see a tiny creature lying on the ground. I instinctively knew that something was badly wrong and my heart sank to the pit of my stomach. When I picked it up, I saw that it was a baby Blue Tit only a few weeks old. There were no obvious signs of life and I felt sure that there was no hope for it. I cupped it in my hands and immediately invoked the angels of healing. I also sent out a plea to St. Francis to restore this tiny creature to life. After thirty minutes of cradling the bird, massaging its tiny frame and surrounding it with pure love and healing energy, there was at last a sign of life. The little bird suddenly stretched its wings and a few moments later flew back to the nest. That afternoon we saw quite a few of its relatives fluttering over and around our pond. We felt it was their way of saying thank you. Both the bird and I received a deep and meaningful demonstration of therapeutic touch that day and I truly feel that my prayers were most definitely answered.

Always

Near

Guiding

Everyone

Like

Stars

Finding my Way

When I first began to work with clients, I felt somewhat daunted by the thought of charging for the treatments, as at that time there seemed to be no formal structure to them. I had no formal qualification in it and at that time there were no books or courses on Therapeutic channelling available in my area. I prayed on it for some time and eventually I sensed that I was to be an 'open book' and to work from my heart centre and my intuition. This I did from a place of trust and I never looked back as they say.

The first few treatments I did on others went well and the clients assured me that they experienced something. They were not at that point too sure what it was, but they felt that it was very soothing, peaceful, and positive. Several of them have said they felt 'embraced by Jesus' while others have said they have seen Mary Magdalene kneeling beside me while I worked on their feet. This is not because I am more spiritual or highly evolved than anyone else, these beings make themselves available to anyone who asks for, or offers healing with an open heart.

The use of oils in my work is not recent either. Throughout my nursing career I have always used oils to massage patient's hands and feet. When a patient in my care did not respond to conventional drug treatments or appeared anxious, restless or in pain, I would offer to massage their hands and feet. They found the application of the oils to have a soothing and calming influence, which improved their overall comfort and general well-being. I also found that using massage with my terminally ill patients brought them comfort and eased their pain, helping them to sleep more peacefully.

My personal experiences and insecurities caused me to doubt the validity of my work at first. I felt like the 'new kid on the block.' It was such a totally different experience from my work as a nurse in which everything in my day was 'structured' and we had to work within clearly defined parameters. I was now working 'blind' and each treatment became and still is an act of faith. Before each treatment I would take time to prepare. I would sit in silent prayer for fifteen minutes or so asking that the client receive the highest level of healing possible. I still use the same prayer today it goes as follows:

My Daily Prayer To God

Holy Father/Mother God, I ask you for a fresh outpouring of the Holy Spirit. I ask for the support for Lord Jesus, Mother Mary, St. Francis, St. Clare, St. Colette, Mary Magdalene, The Archangels Michael, Gabriel, Raphael, Uriel, and Metatron. I also ask all healing angels, Guardian Angels, and all guides who work for the Divine light to assist us this day. I ask to be cleansed of all impurities and strengthened in this healing work. I now invite, invoke, and ask that I be blessed by God and prepared as a channel of Divine love for the highest good of all concerned.

Always

Nice

Generous

Enfolding

Loving

Smiling

Checking it Out

All of my life I have accepted the communications I have received in trust.

A few years ago (2002) I received and noted the information for the Divine Blueprint. This was later to be defined as the Celestial Bagua working with the Four Spheres of Angels, connecting to them with specific colours. I was told that a specific colour was assigned to each of the four Archangel Princes. Michael was to be blue, Gabriel was to be green, Uriel was to be yellow/gold and Raphael was to be red.

Sometime after this I read a book about angels and the Archangels colours differed to those I had been given. I was very confused and doubted myself. I felt like I had been duped. A friend advised me to challenge my guides and the angels and ask for an explanation of the discrepancy. So, I went into the small room I use when I wish to meditate or just sit in silence for a little while and this is the reply I received.

"The Bagua and Healing Trigram were given to you as sacred tools to help yourself and others create beautiful gardens which soothe both the physical, mental, and emotional bodies. They are beneficial to all but most especially to those coping with extreme stress or mental illness. Your breakthrough from illness back to health came after using these colours

and working in your garden daily. At the time they were essential to your return to health. The Bagua remains a valid healing tool that will benefit all who use it. Because you sought safety and solace in you garden, it was a fitting way to connect with you. Using plants in these colours in the appropriate section of the garden created an overall sense of well-being and balance.

When you focus on the colour blue, you connect with Mother Earth. Her maternal healing energies have helped you to become attuned to nature. Your love of trees, Tree Devas, and Elementals has come about as a result of this nurturing. The green strengthened your connection to the healing energy. The yellow/gold helped you to connect more strongly with your divine nature/higher self and the red/pink assisted your emotional healing process.

I am very grateful to the angels for their response, and I trust it. It has been a valuable lesson and I now always ask for clarity as I go along and always use discernment. If it does not feel right, I do not accept it. The guides encourage the questioning and are very supportive of it.

Look for Sean's new book:
Creating An Oasis for Angels
Published by PublishAmerica, Spring of 2005

Angels

Now

Give

Everlasting

Love

Supreme

Doing a Treatment

In my treatment room I have a small table on which I place a white candle to represent the presence of Jesus. I have a small vase of fresh flowers, a piece of clear quartz crystal, a small statue of an angel and an incense boat in which I burn pure incense. In the background soft relaxing music is played to help sooth the client and create a relaxing atmosphere. I give a brief explanation of what I am about to do and ask their permission to begin. You will find the instructions for the sixty-minute treatment on page 70.

Sometimes clients are so 'zapped' by the energies that they need to lie down and rest or even sleep for a little while. This is because sometimes the work can trigger a release of painful memories associated with child abuse or past life traumas and it takes the body a little time to re-balance.

Delivery of the treatment is simple and very pure. My spiritual preparation beforehand is vitally important for both the client and myself. It ensures that there are no negative/impure energies to affect the treatment or the client's healing process. I continue to be guided by and work from my heart.

I have spent many hours learning about how different colours and fragrances work together. More recently I have been learning more about the chakra system and the aura. This led me to try out different ways of using the energy during a therapy. I now use the heart and crown chakras, instead of the thymus and crown chakras, as I find the results more powerful. These findings have been borne out by some of our other therapists. The energy will go where it is needed most. It is safe non-invasive, pain free with no known side effects. It can help to touch and heal core issues that separate us from God and help us reconnect with our Divinity. It is there for anyone to use if they have openness and a willing heart.

I have given this letter from a client I have known for a while a page of its own because I feel that the verse at the end it so apt.

Dear Sean,

How good it was to see you and how blessed I was by your ministrations to me. I pray that your work will go from strength to strength and that many will find renewal and rebirth with your help and guidance.

I value your prayers and feel surrounded and upheld by prayer—what a wonderful power it is. I was reminded of the words of a hymn after your visit.

"But his angels here are human,
Not the shimmering hallows above.
And the drumbeats of His army,
Are the heartbeats of our love."

A. F. - Preston, Lancs.

In a Nut Shell

I believe that Therapeutic Channelling is—

Connecting us with the Divine through touch.
It is a sacred tool that amplifies the healing process.
It empowers us to see God in our daily activities.
It empowers us to self-heal all that is broken within us.
It releases angel energies to assist us to connect with our
     wounded inner child and to release all negative
     thought patterns, painful memories any anything that
     does not serve our 'highest good.'
Therapeutic Touch empowers us to reclaim the healing
     energies of Lord Jesus and see ourselves as children of
     God.
The Divine energies assist us in working with the angelic
     realms.
It is a sacred tool given to you by God.

ANGELS AND REFERENCE

Note from the Author

This book is first and foremost about my own experience of therapeutic touch and healing with the angels.

There has been much written on the subject of angels, but for those who may not yet have discovered these wonderful beings, I have included some basic information on chakras and auras. I have also put in some reference material about angels and what they do. I hope you will have fun with it. There is also a meditation to meet your Guardian Angel and another where your Guardian will give you a Therapeutic Touch session. It is my sincere hope that you will enjoy and be helped by them.

For those who wish to make a more in depth study of angels, I have listed some of my favourite books in the bibliography and recommended reading sections.

Sean

A Typical Angel Day

An angel day begins with a short welcome talk where I introduce myself and give participants a brief idea of what we will do during the day. Then we begin the workshop. The first thing I ask is "What do you hope to get out of the day." I am always amazed at the variety of answers that I get to this question. Participants are invited to share throughout the day, but only if they feel completely comfortable doing so.

Music is played to help everyone relax and to start the energies building up. I then burn incense in an incense boat, which I use to cleanse and purify each corner of the room. I then invite and invoke the Archangel Princes of the Celestial Bagua to join us. Once everyone is ready, we do a meditation to meet our Guardian Angels. This is a very gentle experience that many find very moving. After everyone is properly grounded, I put them into small groups to discuss how they felt about their experience of the meditation. Then we break for lunch.

After lunch we begin some inner child work using the angelic energies. This helps us locate and release problem issues. I then demonstrate the anointing of the feet with blessed oils. The group then split up into pairs and massage each other's feet. (This is also optional as some people do not like their feet to be touched.) If they prefer they can have their hands done instead.

This is followed by a short rest, and then I guide a

meditation to meet the Archangel Princes. When everyone is grounded and fully present, we have questions/sharing. We close the day with the very moving Candle Ceremony mentioned in the chapter on Therapeutic Touch.

I find that the day creates a real bond among the group. The trust and sharing promotes a feeling of safety where, under the guidance of the angels, they can open to their inner healer. People often say to me that they arrive as strangers but leave as friends.

OILS

The carrier oil I use is extra virgin olive oil. I then add Spikenard, eucalyptus, rosemary and grains of frankincense. Spikenard has been used for thousands of years and is revered as a healing tool. It is renowned for its ability to open up the heart centre and clear doubts.

The oil is poured onto the palms of the hands. We then invoke the Archangel Princes and ask them to bless the oils. It is then used to anoint the hands and feet of the client. The heat from both my hands and the client's feet cause the essence of the oils to be released promoting and amplifying the healing energy. Many clients find the experience 'blissful,' while others feel that they are in a dream-like state at the time and report later that things had 'shifted' during the night while they slept, leaving then feeling energised and peaceful.

INCENSE

The use of incense has an equally long history. There is historic evidence in many cultures of its use as a healing tool to deepen meditation, induce a state of calmness, and to heighten spiritual awareness. It is also used to cleanse the room or the 'space' in preparation for healing and meditation.

I would advise the use of good quality (preferably organic) products where possible, as some products are full of synthetic substance that can also be toxic. I use Terra Santa incenses (see useful info) my favourites are Guardian Angel, which lifts the spirit and helps to induce contact with the angels and Rosa Mystica, which helps open up the heart, and help us reconnect with the energies of love.

THE CANDLE CEREMONY

Candles have been used as a source of artificial Light for centuries. They are also used in many rituals and religious services of Divine worship. During my angel healing day workshops, participants are invited to celebrate their lives and their gifts. They are given a brief explanation of the symbolic significance of the use of candles, incense, and blessed oils, which will be used throughout the day.

I believe that the lighting of a candle is a celebration of who we are as children of God. So when we each light our candle at the ceremony, it is a tangible expression of our love for the angelic realm and our God. I see this as an important part of our destiny as light workers.

In many Catholic and High Anglican churches worshippers are invited to light a candle as an expression of their belief in, and devotion to God, the Saints and Angels. It is an act of reverence to The Divine. People often light a candle in petition for favours needed or as a thank you to God and the angels for blessings already received.

When I light my candle at the start of the Angel healing day, it is a symbolic act to represent my love and my commitment to serve the Divine in any way I can as a healer, teacher, and therapist. I place two paintings, one of the Archangel Metatron and the other of Source Angel, on a table at the front of the room. I then place lighted candles in front of them. This helps me clear my mind and my attention becomes clearly focused on the day ahead. When I light the candles, I can feel the angels draw close ready to offer their healing and support to everyone present.

When each participant places their candle in front of the painting of the Archangel Metatron they are invited to take an Angel card if they wish. They then return to their seats and reflect in the silence and the stillness. The atmosphere can become highly charged and is not unknown for several people to experience the presence of angels performing 'hands on healing' during the actual candle ceremony. The ceremony is simple, beautiful, and tranquil. It empowers individuals to release negative thought patterns and painful memories that have sometimes affected their lives for many years. This is followed by a meditation to meet one's God/ess and release the wounded inner child to the light.

During my quiet times before God in meditation and prayer there are moments when I become preoccupied with minutiae. Looking at a lighted candle helps me to re-focus my attention and find solace in the stillness. I also light a candle when I request healing or assistance for others.

INVOCATION

Invocations—invite angels to communicate directly and act through you (channelling).

Evocation—invites the angels/spirits to take on form and show them selves to us.

When I do a one to one session or a workshop I make an invocation to the Archangel Princes. It is as follows:

The invocation is spoken out loud. Whilst making the invocation, I cleanse the room and amplify the healing energy by incensing each direction as I speak. This also forms a circle of protection around everyone in the room.

Facing north I invite and invoke Michael, who is the Archangel Prince of the north, by saying, "I now call upon

55

you Archangel Michael and ask that you now bless, protect, strengthen, and speak to each one of us here today. I thank you Archangel Michael for coming to us during this healing day."

Then facing east I invite and invoke Uriel, who is the Archangel Prince of the east, by saying, "I now call upon you Archangel Uriel and ask that you now bless, protect, strengthen, and speak to each one of us here today. I thank you Archangel Uriel for coming to us during this healing day."

Next I face south and invite and invoke Gabriel, who is the Archangel Prince of the south, by saying, "I now call upon you Archangel Gabriel and ask that you now bless, protect, strengthen, and speak to each one of us here today. I thank you Archangel Gabriel for coming to us during this healing day."

Then I face the west and invite and invoke Raphael, who is the Archangel Prince of the west, by saying, "I now call upon you Archangel Raphael and his team of healing angels and ask that you now bless, protect, strengthen, and speak to each of us here today. I thank you Archangel Raphael for coming to us during this healing day."

Next I face up to the heavens and, still using the incense, I invite and invoke the Archangel Metatron who stands in the presence of Source by saying, "I now call upon you Archangel Metatron and ask that you bless, protect, strengthen, and speak to each of us here today. I thank you for coming to us during this healing day."

Finally I look towards the Earth and invite the fairies, divas, and elementals using the same invocation.

We conclude the induction ritual by cleansing the crown chakra of each participant with incense. Incense is then directed towards the angel paintings thanking them for their love and blessings.

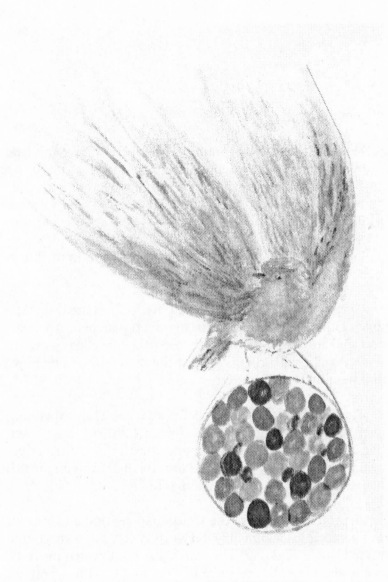

Feedback

Here are a few of the many testimonials I have received from those who have attended an Angel Day.

Therapeutic Touch is for me a coming together with trust between two people to know you feel loved and safe. – Bernie, Mullingar.

I can now begin to see the purpose of Angels in my life as a therapist and healer. – John, England

During the hands on approach my feelings are: I feel the love of the Divine God/ess in my heart—its as if my heart and soul are one, bursting with love so strong all you want to do is share it with clients so that they to can find great love and happiness. - Kath, UK

The benefits are that the client can relax. They experience deep peace within themselves, which helps them restore their lives. They can learn to trust and thereby love themselves again and with this comes the love of their God/ess, which helps us to love all people again. – Robie, UK

To protect the gifts of the sacred energies that are inherent in Therapeutic Channelling, I have discovered how to 'ground myself' night and day! The course has empowered me to be silent and listen to the sacred voices and be still. I pray for spiritual guidance in my sacred place and often through the day. My physical, spiritual and mental balance I work on by praying and asking the Angels of the Healing Bagua and the Trigram to help me while I grow and sow God's seeds. – M, Ireland.

I have been moved to the point of tears for the years spent in selfish activity and denial of my true feelings and needs as a Healer and Therapist. Now I can see for the very first time and can really enjoy working with these sacred energies in the knowledge that I AM LOVED unconditionally. – Sally M, Blackpool.

As a channeller working in partnership with Metatron, Source, and the entire angelic realms, I know that I am loved— chosen and called by name to touch others in the name of selfless love divine. Thank you. – Maria, Cumbria UK.

This course has been a tonic! It has challenged me to look at myself and face the hurts and brokenness that have prevented me from living life to the full as a human being and as a therapist. – Joe, London UK.

Meetings Between Guardian Angels

Consider the closest thing to an angel on
    earth—your mind or soul.
In the blink of an eye, in your mind—
    Which is spirit like an angel—
You can go from the room you were married
    in to the edge of the universe.
Being spirits, angels move like our
    imaginations—instantly,
As near or as far as they want,
To the past, present or future.

John Ronner

Meeting Your Companion/Guardian Angel (CD/Book Angelic Energies)

Find a place where you feel warm, safe, and comfortable. You may wish to create a prayer corner with some fresh flowers, crystals, and a white candle. You could burn some incense if you wish (these things help to create the tight atmosphere for connecting with your Angels).

Now I invite you to join me in a very special journey to meet your companion/guardian Angel...Just allow yourself to relax, and let go of any tension that may be present in your body...bring your attention to your breathing...notice the steady, even rhythm...just know that as you breathe in, you breathe in unconditional love...and as you breath out, you are letting go of all of your stress and worries...any problems or difficult situations you have to deal with...(repeat suggestions for about 6-7 breaths)...

Now as you breathe in, you notice that momentary pause between the in breath, and the out breath...and the pause between the out breath, and the in breath...You let your attention shift to the pause, and just sit in that stillness...you feel totally relaxed and at peace.

Now see yourself walking calmly through a field...You are enjoying the gentle breeze, and the bright warm sunshine...You notice a wooded area up ahead and decide to spend some time among the trees...As you enter the wood, you sense the presence of the angels of nature, the tree divas, and the fairies welcoming you into their domain...You feel a deep joy and contentment...You stroll through the woods, enjoying the colours, and scents of the flowers, the sounds of the birds singing...and the rustling of the leaves.

You come to a clearing and notice that in the middle of it, there is a beautiful building with a big oak door...

As you come to the edge of the clearing and glance down, you notice some steps cut into the side of the slope...You walk slowly down the steps, (countdown if you wish)...and along the path to the door...as you arrive at the door, it opens and you walk through it into a hallway with a beautiful spiral staircase, which appears to be made entirely of exquisite rainbow light...You gaze at it wonder and you begin to sense a presence like a fine mist, floating down the stairs towards you...As you watch it approach, you have a deep sense of calm and peace.

The mist dissolves, and from it appears the most radiantly beautiful being you have ever seen...Look into their eyes and feel the unconditional love radiating from them, you know to the deepest level of you being that you are totally loved and accepted exactly as you are...(pause for a few minutes)—(I would give occasional gentle encouragement to just feel that unconditional love fill every cell of body)...

The angel takes you by the hand, and leads you through a door into a large comfy room...There are two large armchairs, and you both sit down...Once again you look into their eyes and still feeling the love that surrounds you. You may respectfully ask your companions name...(Pause for response)...Now you may ask, if your companion has any message for you

that will help you on your path...(Pause for response)—
(again gentle encouragement)

It is time to leave now, so take a moment to express
your thanks to you companion and say goodbye...again
you are taken by the hand and escorted to the door...If
you wish, you may ask your angel for a hug...Thank
them once again and say goodbye...

As you walk back through the door, it closes behind
you...You walk back along the path and up the steps
(count up if you wish)...and back into the wood...

As you are strolling back through the wood towards
the field...you notice a small stone circle about a meter
in diameter on the ground in front of you...if you wish
you may step into the circle and sit down...close your
eyes...take a few moment to enjoy the stillness...you
sense that someone has joined you...gently open your
eyes and see who it is...ask for a name...is it a fairy...an
elemental...a tree spirit... or someone else...again ask
for any message they have to give you...(pause for a
few minutes)...ask if there is anything you can do for
them...(pause a few minutes)...thank them and say
goodbye.

You step out of the circle, and continue on your way
out of the wood...as you re-enter the field, you realise
you are feeling very energized and refreshed...as you
stroll back through the field you are more and more
awake...when you are ready knowing you will bring
the feeling of peace and acceptance with you, come
back in to the room...

Have everyone stretch themselves out.

This meditation is available on CD. See contacts section
for details.

What do Angels Mean to You

During the Angel Day Workshops, I put participants into small groups and give them questions, which are designed to make then think about what angels mean to them. I am writing them here and invite you think about what the answers are for you personally. I have listed some of the most common replies at the end of the chapter.

Morning Questions –

Question 1:

The word angel comes from the Greek word 'angeloi' meaning messenger. Who do angels bring messages from and to whom?

Question 2:

I believe that angels work alongside me and that they touch my life daily. How do angels touch you?

Question 3:

I believe that angels have helped me transform my life. They have helped me through a major illness and empowered me to be the person that I am today. How can angels empower you to love and accept yourself?

Question 4:

The Archangel Princes are messengers of the Divine. The role of Metatron is to help us to reclaim our 'first love.' Who is our first love and what does it mean to you?

Question 5:

Explain why you should reclaim your 'first love.' And what benefits this would bring you.

Afternoon questions –

Question 1:

When we open our mind, body, and spirit to embrace our 'higher-self,' we experience something rather beautiful and awesome. In your own words, describe these feelings and emotions.

Question 2:

The being called source has already met up with us in a time before we were born. Explain why you feel this to be true, or false.

Question 3:

In your own words, please explain the meaning of the phrase 'Physician heal thyself,' and why it is so important for you today.

Question 4:

Facing life's hurts and traumas can indeed be challenging. Why is it so important for you as an adult to connect with your inner child?

The Most Common Answers to Both the Morning and Afternoon Questions.

Morning Questions

Question 1:

Angels bring messages to anyone in need.
There are no restrictions.
Angels administer Divine love in gentleness and joy.
Those who can change things.
Those who are open to change.
Angels are messengers of diversity.
The soul creator within us.

Question 2:

They give us wisdom and clarity.
They touch our lives through our children.
Ask and you shall receive.
They are always around to help especially when we are at
    a crossroads in our lives.
Things that appear to be co-incidences.
Through our inner voice.

Question 3:

A presence, someone there when we experience our lowest

moments.

At one and feeling empowered.

When I falter, or fall short of what is expected of me by
others, my angel sends me 'balls of golden light.'

To be able to give love we need to have felt true love.

Connecting to this loves gives me strength.

Angels touch us through other people.

Angels will help you find things as well as parking spaces.

Angels touch us in our dreams.

I feel like I have been enveloped in love.

Question 4:

My first love is me.

My first love is the light from which I came.

Our first love is our self. Our higher self—our spiritual
forms.

We are all energy.

When you love yourself, you love all.

Recognising the Divine in me.

My first love is Source.

I believe that my first love is the divine spark within me
that is connected—has always been so and is God the
soul.

Question 5:

Life is precious; go out and embrace life—compassion.

By looking directly into the flames of Divine love, we can
see only pure love.

We are all one spirit, connected to the light, the place we
all call home.

She brings comfort when alone.

Be myself, love myself, connect with the I AM in the NOW.

Afternoon Questions.

Question 1:

Alone, balanced, energised, complete, loved, empowered, clarity and wisdom.

When we connect there is an oneness and united in love and peace, share this and spread it, and be still and complete.

I got the image of a broken heart in two clear pieces, all of them being stitched back together with love by unseen hands.

I feel an indescribable sense of peace; being enveloped in a sense of perfection and balance.

White light; presence of more than one, feeling loved and safe.

Question 2:

Source is true, alive and well.

Knowing source gives me a feeling of being loved and protected.

Source gives me a feeling of being a baby cradled in his/her arms.

Circles of white light – shooting to small dots – like stars and then disappearing.

I remember before I came here because he/she sits in my heart centre because he/she wraps me in comfort.

Question 3:

If you cannot help yourself you cannot help others.

To go on a journey and heal the hurt and damaged child within. To recognise the ability to heal oneself, to be

honest with yourself and to find and hold peace.
Self worth.
We have a responsibility to our spiritual selves to be all
    that we can be, to be whole.
We need to connect with the wounded child within to leg
    go and to heal.
We are responsible for our own lives.

Question 4:

Freedom from shame, recognising and rejoicing in our
    specialness.
Recognising our inner beauty.
An acceptance of all that is presented to you.
To make us stronger and more 'whole.'
To be free of any negative beliefs that are holding me back.

A Therapeutic Treatment

A one to one therapeutic treatment usually lasts for 60 minutes. Before you start, I recommend that you make sure the room is warm and free of draughts. Play some soft music and keep the lighting in the room very soft.

1. A brief introduction to the session (5 minutes)
2. Take a brief summary of the client's details (name, tel no, etc - 5 minutes)
3. Seat client in an upright position and assist them to relax. Make sure they feel comfortable and safe.
4. In silence, place both your hands on the client's head. (crown chakra) and quietly invoke the four Archangel Princes. (Michael, Gabriel, Raphael and Uriel) Hold hands in this position for 5 to 8 minutes.
5. Position yourself facing the right side of the client. Gently place your left hand on the client's head and at the same time place your right hand on the client's heart chakra. Again invite, invoke, and ask the four Archangel Princes together with all four spheres of angelic servers to come and assist you now in this treatment. Continue these hand positions for at least 10 minutes.
6. Following this sacred attunement exercise, ask your client to remove their shoes, socks, etc. Invite the client to lie on a treatment couch or sit in a chair, whichever is most comfortable for them. Place a towel

under their feet and legs.

7. Gently encourage the client to relax and observe the rhythm of their breathing.

8. Ask your client to visualise themselves resting in a safe place. Then working from the client's head to the tips of their toes, encourage them to be willing to let go of any negative thought patterns they may have and just relax (guided meditation for relaxation)

9. Apply some sacred oil to your hands and using gentle downward strokes, massage the client's lower leg from knee to ankle, then to the tips of their toes. (Have client visualise the angels taking any negativity out through their feet and recycling it into light. (10 minutes each foot)

10. Positive energy is being poured down through the crown chakra. It flows all around the body filling the places where negativity was with pure love. (Continue for 10 minutes)

11. Assure client is comfortable and relaxed.

12. Ask the client to place both their hands on a towels placed over their abdominal area.

13. Taking one hand at a time, place some of the sacred oil and massage it gently into their hands and wrist. (5 minutes each hand)

14. Encourage the clients to relax and allow themselves to absorb the healing energy. (Allow another 5 minutes)

15. When this process feels complete, gently encourage the client to come back to the present and when they are ready they can open their eyes. Assist them to put on their shoes.

It is strongly recommended that clients should rest for a short while and drink a large glass of water before they leave, especially if they are driving a car.

The client should be reminded to drink plenty of water in the days following a treatment (at least 2 litres a day, more if possible) as it will help to flush toxins out of the client's body.

I found this lovely poem whilst I was browsing the Internet one afternoon. The author is unknown, but I thank him or her anyway. I would like to share it with you.

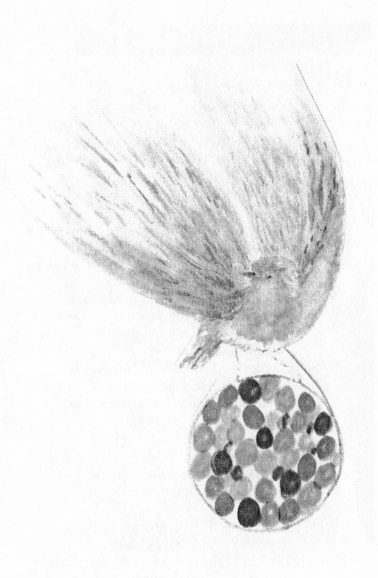

What do Angels Look Like?

Like the little old lady who returned
your wallet yesterday.
Like the taxi driver who told you that your eyes
light up the world when you smile.
Like the small child who showed you
the wonder in simple things.
Like the poor man who offered to
share his lunch with you.
Like the rich man who showed you that it was really
all possible, if only you believe.
Like the stranger who just happened to come along,
when you had lost your way.
Like the friend who touched your heart,
when you didn't think you had one to touch.
Angels come in all sizes and shapes,
all ages and skin types.
Some with freckles, some with dimples,
some with wrinkles, some without.
They come disguised as friends, enemies,
teachers, students, lovers and fools.
They don't take life too seriously,
they travel light.
They leave no forwarding address,
they ask nothing in return.

They wear sneakers with gossamer wings,
they get a deal on dry cleaning.
They are hard to find when your eyes are closed,
but they are everywhere you look,
When you choose to see.

Author Unknown

74

Creating the Right Atmosphere

Although it is possible to meditate almost anywhere, some people find it helps to have a special place where they can relax and let go of the stresses of the day.

There are some things you can do to help create a peaceful space. You can create an altar using some of the following things. They are not essential, but it helps to surround yourself with beautiful things such as pictures, ornaments, fresh flowers, and candles. All of the following things should be chosen intuitively. Select the ones that 'speak' to you.

FLOWERS
Fresh ones are best, but you can use good quality silk ones and scent them with oils. A cheaper alternative is to use potted plants, which last much longer and you can use ones, which will flower regularly.

INCENSE

You can burn incense if you like. This will help to cleanse the room of any negative energy. Try and get a good quality organic incense if you can as it is much more effective than the cheaper varieties.

To purify a room use— sandalwood, frankincense, or cedar
For relaxation try—lavender, lemongrass, or rose.

CANDLES

White

A white candle draws our angels to us. It symbolizes spiritual energy, peace, truth, sincerity, and power. When a white candle is burned alongside another colour, it amplifies the properties of the other colour.

Red

Promotes passion, courage, strength, and desire.

Orange

Promotes creativity, kindness, compassion, and adaptability.

Yellow

Promotes clairvoyance, confidence, attraction, and imagination.

Green

Promotes luck, fertility, healing, and personal growth.

Light blue

Promotes tranquility, devotion, harmony in relationships, and patience.

Indigo

Promotes openness, ambition, helps to diminish compulsive behavior, and can assist in developing ESP.

Violet

Helps to clear sadness, depression, and guilt. It promotes spiritual growth and like indigo it helps with the development of ESP.

If you are doing any healing work on your chakras, you can burn a candle in the relevant colour and a white one to increase its power.

Other useful colours are—

Purple

Helps with spiritual growth, abundance, fighting infection, and increasing ambition.

Pink

Is for love, honour, increased understanding of a situation, and strengthens friendships.

OILS

If you don't like incense or find it irritating (a few of my clients find it irritates their throats), you may prefer to use an oil burner to scent the room.

There are many different oils to choose from, but I have listed a few of my favorites below.

Relaxing

Lavender, bergamot, jasmine, patchouli, rose, and ylang-ylang.

Stimulating

Eucalyptus, lemongrass, myrrh, peppermint, pine, and tea tree.

Uplifting

Bergamot, orange, lemon balm (melissa officinalis), lavender, juniper, and geranium.

CRYSTALS

Crystals are not only very beautiful to look at, they also enhance the energy in a room. They can help you to focus and to rebalance. Once again if you are buying one choose the one that draws you to it.

Calming

Clear Quartz, citrine, rose quartz, amethyst, and tiger's eye.

Balancing

Clear quartz, smoky quartz, rose quartz, aventurine, and amethyst.

Protection

Jasper and tourmaline

Grounding

Jasper and clear quartz

Energizing

Bloodstone, carnelian, and citrine.

Relaxing

Chrysophrase, rose quartz, and amethyst.

Healing

Ritulated quartz, rose quartz, and amethyst

Cleansing

Smoky quartz.

A Visualization of Therapeutic Touch from Your Companion/Guardian Angel (CD/Book Angelic Energies)

Find a place where you feel warm, safe, and comfortable. You may wish to create a prayer corner with some fresh flowers, crystals and a white candle. You could burn some incense if you wish. (These things help create the right atmosphere for connecting with your angels)

Now I invite you to join me on a very special journey to meet your companion/guardian Angel...Just allow yourself to relax, and let go of any tension that may be present in your body...now bring your attention to your breathing...notice the steady, even rhythm...just know that as you breathe in, you breath in unconditional love...and as you breathe out, you are letting go of all your stress...any problems, or difficult situations you have to deal with...(gentle suggestion for 6-7 breaths)...just breathe in pure love...breathe out stress and tension...with each breath you feel calmer...Take another deep slow breath...now as you breath in, notice the momentary pause between the in breath, and the our breath...and the pause between the out breath, and the in breath...You let your attention shift to the pause...just relax into the stillness...you feel totally relaxed and at peace.

It is time to revisit the beautiful place you were in before and meet once again with your companion angel...see yourself walking once again through the field towards the wood...It feels safe and familiar as you have travelled this path before...you walk through the woods once again enjoying the sights, sounds, and smells of nature...You come to the clearing...and once again notice the beautiful building with the big oak door.

You come to the edge of the clearing...and walk slowly down the steps. (countdown if you wish)...and along the path to the door...As you arrive at the door, it opens and you walk through it into the hallway...at the bottom of the spiral staircase, which appears to be made entirely of exquisite rainbow coloured light...as you gaze at it, you sense that there is a presence like a fine mist...floating down the stairs towards you...as you watch it approach...you experience a deep sense of peace...The mist dissolves, and from it appears the radiantly beautiful being you met that last time you visited this magical place...Look into their eyes and feel the unconditional love radiating from them...you know to the deepest level of your being, that you are totally loved and accepted, exactly as you are...just relax and rest in that love...(pause for a minute)...feel the peace...the gentleness...the stillness...as you absorb the pure healing energies into every cell of your body.

The angel takes you by the hand and leads you up the stairway of light and into a crystal healing room...in the distance you can hear a choir of angels singing...The angel leads you gently to a comfy sofa in the centre of the room...and invites you to lie down...(if you prefer you may sit in the a chair that has been placed next to it.)...A soft warm blanket is placed over you, and you feel warm...cosy...comfortable...safe...as you rest a while...(short pause) and look around you, you notice the rays of healing light shining all around you...You feel peaceful and sink further into the stillness.

As you lay resting in that stillness...the angel approaches and asks if he may waft some incense around the room...if you prefer not to have incense in the room...just remain in the stillness...if you do want it...just relax as he lights the incense to cleanse the room...you are totally at peace...resting in the pure love, ready to receive this special healing.

Your companion now invites the four Archangel princes Michael, Raphael, Uriel, and Gabriel to join him...and you look on in wonder as they appear at the four corners of the sofa...feel their love flow into you...

The angel stands behind you and places both hands gently on your head...experience the warmth as the healing energy flows into your body...Michael steps forward and bathes you in healing lights...of the most beautiful shades of blue...relax for a minute and allow yourself to absorb them...Uriel steps forward and adds his beautiful shades of yellow, gold, and orange...again you relax and absorb them...Gabriel adds his energy, the most glorious shades of green...just allow yourself to soak in these wonderful rays...Raphael joins the others, and adds his wonderful pinks and reds...Now allow yourself to bask for a few minutes in this glorious serene, healing love...(music for 2 minutes)

Your companion is still working on your crown, and now moves a hand down to your heart chakra...you can feel the warmth, radiating from their hands...you feel totally balanced and at peace...(pause 2 mins)

The angel now moves to the bottom of the couch...and places a soft towel under your feet...The Archangel princes form a circle of healing light around you, you can still see the exquisite rainbow colours that fill the room...you experience their love, and protection at the deepest levels of you being...

Your companion is now kneeling beside you in silence...and pours the blessed oils into their hands...the angel asks a blessing on the oils, and everyone involved in this special healing...you just relax and enjoy the feelings, as your companion massages the oil, into you lower right leg...working in a slow and graceful motion from your knee to the tips of you toes...(music 1 minute)...

Your companion now moves to your left leg...now you experience the healing touch of the angel's hands...as they massage and soothe...sense the unconditional love flow through your limbs and up through the whole of your body...(music 1 minute)

The angel now works on both feet together, and invites God's blessing on you...then covers your feet with the warm towels...before beginning work on your hands...

Feel your companion, stroking from your right elbow, to the tips of your fingers...gently soothing...(music 1 minute)...now the process is repeated on the left arm...gentle soothing strokes from the elbow to your fingers...(music 1 minute)

The four Archangel princes continue to flood the room, and your entire being with healing, and unconditional love...lie back and feel the total peace and bliss...(music 2 minutes)

Your treatment is now complete, and your companion expresses their thanks with a respectful bow...this wonderful being acknowledges your perfection as a child of God...You are invited to join in giving thanks to the Archangel princes...(short pause)...

Your companion takes you by the hand and escorts you back down the staircase of light and across the hall to the door…If you wish, you may ask your angel for a hug…Thank them once again and say goodbye…As you out through the door, it closes behind you…you walk back along the path and up the steps…(count up if you want to)…and back through the wood.

As you are strolling back through the wood you realise you are feeling refreshed…awake…energised…as you re-enter the field you are even more awake, confident, at peace…when you are ready, and knowing that you will bring that feeling of peace, and acceptance, back with you…you come back into the room…

When you have completed your meditation, stretch yourself out and drink a large glass of water. This will help to re-hydrate and ground you. As you go about your day, know that your companion is always with you, loving, supporting and guiding.

Love and light,
Sean

A Brief Overview of Angels

The word angel comes from the Greek word 'angelos' meaning messenger. Angels are accepted in many of the main religions including Islam, Judaism, Christianity, and Shinto. They all place a special importance on the presence of angels in their scriptures. I have also met people who do not consider themselves religious at all, who believe they have had an encounter with an angel.

Angels are beings of light. They do not have physical bodies like we do, but they are capable of taking on human form if necessary. They can present themselves as male or female, but in reality they are a perfect balance of both.

There are angels for everything, birth, death, study, and even things like parking the car. I believe we each have a guardian angel that stays with us for our whole lifetime. We can ask for angelic assistance with any problem we face or task we have to do. They are always there to comfort us when we are ill or just feeling down and unable to cope. Every request or prayer is answered without exception.

Below are a few of the ways our angels can talk to us.

Synchronicity

Our attention is drawn to a book, film or person who can help us or we may 'just happen' to overhear a conversation which gives or helps us find the answer we need. We need to aware and watch for the 'clues.'

Dowsing

You could use a pendulum to dowse for the answers. Before you begin ask the pendulum/dowser to show you a yes answer and then a no answer. With me, for yes the pendulum moves in a clockwise circular motion, and for no, it goes back and forth, or side to side. It can vary from person to person, so take a little time to found out what works for you. Remember to phrase your questions so they can be answered with a yes or a no.

Automatic writing

Invoke your Guardian and ask for their assistance. Write your question at the top of a piece of paper then relax and just let your hand go. Try to keep you mind clear and do not think about or judge what comes till you are finished. If you do not feel comfortable or you are receiving negative communication, then stop immediately.

Angel cards

There are many beautiful sets of angel cards on the market at the moment. I particularly like the *Mermaid and Dolphin Cards* by Doreen Virtue and her *Messages from Your Angels Cards*. I find that cards are a bit like crystals, they tend to choose us. See which ones speak to you.

You can also contact them psychically. This is a skill that anyone can develop with a little practice. If you decide to look for a teacher to help you, yet again, choose intuitively.

Your angel friends may manifest a white feather to show you that they have heard your call and are around you. I believe they can also take on the form of birds to show us they have heard us and to bring us comfort. I believe an angel in the form of a Robin visited me some years ago while I worked in my garden. I was feeling very low at the time as I had been working hard and had many painful things going on in my life. I feel that it was my Guardian bringing me comfort and hope.

The Order of Angelic Beings
Watching Over Us

Research from around the world tells us that from the beginning of time we have had celestial representation. Our ancestors have fuelled our imagination with stories of things that inspired them to believe in the existence of these magical beings. I believe that there are angels for every task and purpose from birth and death to parking the car. The following poems are a tribute to departed friends and the Angels who care for them.

A poem for a friend called Tish who had an angel heart.

"When you came for me and took me by the hand,
you whispered to me of another land...
you told me how my pain would be at ease...
and how my mortal suffering would cease.
You stroked my cheek and softly promised, true,
That if I simply said "I will" to you...
That you would take me from this fearful pain...
And let me live as once I had again...
When I was strong and loud and full of love...
And took of life without reprove.
I never thought that there would come a time
When health, and strength would not be,
By Divine right, mine.
Oh you tempt me with your soft and velvet voice...
You seduce me without hinting I have choice...
But Death I look you in the face and say;
I choose to do this my way.
I am not ready to take your hands,
Nor listen to your talk of other lands...
I still have things I want to do and say...
And I so choose to go my way...
YES, my pain is real and cuts me deep...
And YES the cancer grows...
And YES I weep,
But save your whispers for another day,
And take your cool and tempting hands away,
For when I choose to reach and take your hand,
I do it willingly, not on demand.

Written for Tish Clifford who left us in 1994 by her friend
Alison.

Angels of God

Angels of God are close beside YOU
Waiting in love
They are there to guide you.
When you ASK them to help you,
They will shower you with love
because they already know you.

Seek first their path to true peace and joy
And know that they will sustain you
The Child of God you truly are.
Believe in your heart that when you summon them,
They will come to bless your life
For ever more.
Angels of God are here to stay,
so rest assured that they are with you now
All the way.

Sean Bradley

Dedicated to Ellen Ann an angel of God who passed away
in 2002.

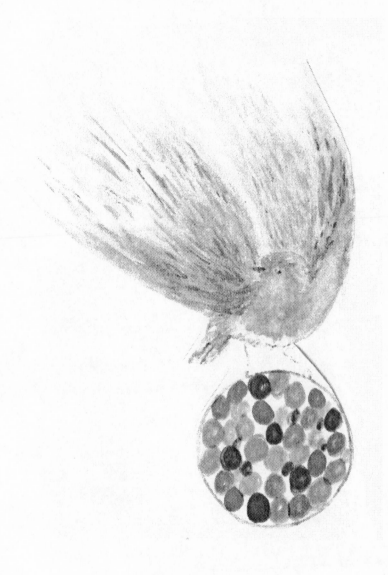

HIERARCHY

Hierarchy

First Sphere

1 Seraphim
Seraphim are said to be the closest to God and the most highly evolved of the angels. They sing the music of the spheres that holds everything in the Universe in balance.

2 Cherubim
Cherubim are the guardians of light. They send us Divine light from the heavens and maintain the bridge of light between the planes, which enables us to have mystical/higher experiences in safety.

3 Thrones
The Thrones are the guardian/companion angels of planets. The Throne who cares for the Earth works to create a balance between species and to prevent or reduce the effects of disasters.

Second Sphere

4 Dominions
Dominions are angelic governors who serve to integrate the material and spirit worlds. They help the guardian angels look after the person to whom they are assigned.

5 Virtues

Virtues send spiritual energy to the planet. They are able to send huge amounts of Divine energy at any time. They listen to our requests for healing and our prayers and respond appropriately.

6 Powers

Powers are the keepers of our history. They hold the energy of the Divine plan and bear the conscience of humanity. They are also keepers of the Akashic Records.

Third Sphere

7 Principalities

Principalities care for large groups, such as large companies and corporations, and even whole cities and nations.

8 Archangels

These beings are different from angels. They work to bring clarity and light to specific areas of human endeavour. They will when asked bring safety and help us to find clarity about our purpose in life.

9 Angels

Angels are closest to humans. There are many different categories that perform different functions. There are angels for everything and ever purpose and they will always respond to a request or plea for assistance.

The above are the three best-known spheres of angelic beings. However, there is a fourth which has finally been recognised by us they are the angels of nature. It is made up of the Elementals and Tree Devas. I feel the following quote from Flower A Newhouse sums it up.

"Nature, then, is the seedbed out of which the Creator brings forth new generations of Angelic servers. The youngest of these forms of nature beings are called Elementals; tiny entities who permeate the planet and who literally breathe life and health into all that makes up the four natural realms. Each realm, earth, fire, water and air is home to a sequence of beings that ascend towards devahood, the final stage of evolution in becoming an Angel."

Seraphim Call

Brilliant Seraphim I call to thee
Circle round bring love to me.
Mighty Cherubim guard my gate
Remove from me sorrow and hate.
Thrones stand firm, stable be
Keep me steady on land or sea.
I call Dominions, leadership true
May I be fair in all I do.
Circles of protection Powers form
Help me weather every storm.
Miraculous Virtues hover near
Elementals energies I summon here.
Principalities bring global reform
Bless the world and each babe born.
Glorious Archangels show me the way
To bring peace and harmony every day.
Guardian angel, Goddess might
Bless me with your guiding light.

Author Unknown

Named Archangel Princes
of the Angel Magic Square
(Healing Trigram and Angel Bagua)

Angels welcome diversity and so are champions of our individuality, sexuality, ethnicity, religious beliefs, and cultural differences.

When we embrace the angelic realms, particularly when we rediscover the angels of the 'Nature Wave,' they transform our gardens into 'sacred sanctuaries' where God and the angels of the four spheres dwell. This transformation has a knock on effect in our lives as well as our relationships with others. Our spirit is reawakened and our love for God and the angels is no longer dormant but active and creative. I found it hard at first to connect with the angelic realms due to an innate fear and religious superstition handed to me in childhood. However, as with any relationship, I had to learn how to love them and receive their love. It was like being a child in kindergarten or nursery, they had to show me how to be still and let go of any fear. It took a little time, but I soon learned to relax and to 'hear' their communication. At the time I was just coming through a mental illness and doubted what was happening to me and around me. I had been ill. I was no longer able to do my job as a nurse in a busy NHS hospital. I lost my home, my partner of twenty-four years, and my self respect. Thankfully there was light at the end of the tunnel. I was given the courage to ask for and accept their help and the rest as they say is history.

The future had seemed bleak, but I sensed that I was being supported and nurtured by the presence of angels in my garden. I was not a gardener at the time, or an expert in angels or garden design. My tutors were the angles of the nature wave and the animal kingdom. What I learned was not my doing, but theirs. When I think back, I believe I was being prepared to receive the 'Divine Blueprint' known as the Healing Trigram, Angel Bagua, and Celestial Placement Square, although, at the time, it felt as though it had happened within a few months. Through the simple tasks of weeding, pruning, and planting seedlings for the next season's growth, my life was transformed. I feel humbled that they used me to create such beauty.

These gardens have an eclectic feel to them. They incorporate within them the energy of several different cultures and honour God no matter what our individual perception of him may be.

To make that first connection, we have to approach the angelic realms with reverence, humility, and respect. We must communicate with simplicity of heart. When I first became aware that there were divas who supervise the trees, plants, flowers, and the four elements of air, water, fire, earth, I felt that the angels of nature were hesitant to work with man because of the damage done to these kingdoms. Over a period of months, I became increasingly aware of their presence and would often see them working alongside me in the garden. Now when I travel to do workshops, I ask the Divas for their support in the garden. On my return, I am never surprised to find everything is shipshape when I return.

Connecting with the angels of the Earth is not difficult. Our Guardian angels and the Archangels make it as easy for us as possible. You do not have to be religious or a regular churchgoer to access their support. What they look for is sincerity and commitment to embrace God's creation.

According to St. Thomas Aquinas, "Angels transcend every religion, every philosophy, every creed. In fact, angels have no religion as we know it.... their existence precedes every religious system that has ever existed on Earth." Angels represent the Divine and spirituality.

The Creator has entrusted Archangels with unique powers—gifts and specialist skills to place at our disposal and facilitate our relationship with him. Each area of the Angel Bagua—Trigram and Celestial Placement Square has been enriched by God's energies for the benefit of our spiritual, physical, and mental well-being. When we are faced with fear, trauma, illness, depression, or anxiety, we are advised to stop and reflect. Breathe in the peace of the angelic realms and become totally infused with their energy. Angels are truly the messengers of God working tirelessly behind the scenes on our behalf.

To access their energy it is important to know a little about the Archangel Princes, especially who they are and what they do on our behalf. Here is a little information on the Archangels named in the Bagua.

The Named Archangel Princes Are

1. Archangel Michael   -   Prince of the North.

2. Archangel Uriel   -   Prince of the East.

3. Archangel Gabriel   -   Prince of the South.

4. Archangel Raphael   -   Prince of the West

5. Archangel Metatron   -   Prince of the inner circle of universal life

Force energy—angelic energy.

The Named Archangels of the Celestial Magic Placement Square Are:

1. Archangel Michael (North)
2. Archangel Melchizedek (South West)
3. Archangel Uriel (East)
4. Archangel Moroni (South East)
5. Archangel Israfael (Centre)
6. Archangel Raziel (North West)
7. Archangel Raphael (West)
8. Archangel Ariel (North East)
9. Archangel Gabriel (south)
10. Archangel Metatron (Inner Circle)

Archangel Michael

Michael appears to be the most well known of the Archangels and is something of a 'favourite.' The name Michael means "Who is like God," but he is also known by other names and titles, which were given to him because if his unquestioning loyalty and devotion. He is also known as the 'Warrior Angel, Angel of Patience, and Prince of the Chaldeans.' Michael is always there for us and is a powerful spiritual ambassador who will help us throughout our life's journey. Michael is depicted as a 'warrior angel' with sword in hand ready to fight evil. He represents the marginalized as well as the oppressed in our society. Some believe he is the angel responsible for the well being of the heavenly realms. It was Michael who vanquished and hauled the Archangel Lucifer from the Heavens when he tried to take over the Throne of God. The fight between Michael and Lucifer is said to represent the fight between the forces of 'light and darkness,' which is as evident in our world as it was then today, as it was then.

Message from Michael

"Open your heart to receive the love of all Loves. I am your helper and will walk with you each step of the way on your journey through life. Believe that what you experience here on Earth is transitory and will not defeat you. Believe that through life's hurts and disappointments there is hope.

Connect with the Divine that is within you, all around you, and even in the air you breathe. I will assist you in every way possible; you only have to ask and we will come to you. You are a child of God. You were created from God's love. From the moment of inception through conception, you were cherished and loved. Open your heart and we will show you the different ways that you can embrace the Divine. Listen and you will hear God speaking to you through the elements, the beautiful landscapes, and the wildlife. Wherever you are and whatever happens to you, many unseen helpers surround you. You only have to ask."

Archangel Melchizedek

Named the 'Angel of Divine Presence,' he took human form to do the work of God. Biblical scholars have recorded in detail that it was Melchizedek who delivered God's Covenant to Abraham. When a priest is ordained in the Church the sacred rite's of ordination state, "You shall be a priest according to the order of Melchizedek."

Message from Melchizedek

"I bring you the healing love and power of all angels. Living in the modern world has its rewards as well as difficulties. My presence in the angel peace garden will assist you to achieve wholeness and completeness in your relationships with others. If you are searching for a partner who is of like mind, then know I am here and believe that I shall endeavour to bring you together. When you ask for assistance, I will come to you for I see the Divine in you and the innocence. I will offer comfort when your heart is lonely."

Archangel Uriel

Means 'The fire of God.' Uriel is a high angel and is of the Seraphim who are said to be the angels closest to God. His other titles are 'Regent of the Sun, Flame of God, and the Archangel of Salvation.' Uriel is perceived by scholars to be the 'sharpest sighted' angelic spirit in all of Heaven.

Message from Archangel Uriel

"I am your support when all may seem hopeless. My role in the Angel Peace Garden is to come with gifts that will liberate your spirit. I am awaiting your invitation to bring to you the love of the angels and the love of the Nature Kingdom. It is my task to support families in turmoil and help them resolve their difficulties. I come to you and your families in love and wish for your happiness at every level of your existence. True and lasting happiness is achieved when we are at one with each other. You are not alone in your search for fellowship, freedom, contentment, and belonging. I will assist you in your quest for inner fulfilment and spiritual contentment. You are never alone when you embrace the Divine in your sacred oasis.

Archangel Moroni

Known as the 'Angel of Light.' He was the angel that appeared to John Smith in the USA in 1823. He is known as the Angel of the Latter Day Saints (Mormons). It is said that when he appeared to John Smith, he was as a 'Being of light with a face that resembled lightning.'

Message from Archangel Moroni

My assigned area within the Angel Bagua is wealth. The wealth of God's love is a rare and precious thing. It is your birthright and is freely given to all who choose to accept it and invite him into their lives. When you enter your peace garden be aware that you are in the presence of angels and of God. In the silence, feel the power of his peace and his love. God has no wish to see his children in pain; he loves all of you unconditionally. He wishes for all of mankind to live in peace and abundance. It is not evil or unspiritual to be abundant as long as you acquire your wealth honourably. All you have to do is ask, believe, and accept it with love.

Archangel Israfael

Known as the 'Burning One.' According to angelologists, Israfael is said to have paved the way for Gabriel by serving for three years as a companion to Mohammed whom he originally initiated as a prophet. In the Islamic version of Genesis during the account of Adam's creation, Allah sent Israfael, Gabriel, Michael, and Azrael, the Angel of Death, out on a mission to fetch the seven handfuls of dust needed to make Adam. According to legend only Israfael was successful. He is described as the 'four winged' angel. He is described as he whose 'heart strings are as a lute' and he who has the sweetest voice of all God's creatures. It is said that this wonderful Archangel sings the praises of the creator in a thousand different tongues. Israfael is the patron saint of entertainers and artists. It is said that when the world ends, he will descent to Earth and stand on the Holy Rock in Jerusalem and blow the sacred trumpet that will awaken the dead from their slumber and summon all who have ever lived to their judgement day. Scholars say that he looks into Hell three times each day and night, and is stricken with a grief so great that his weeping could flood the Earth with tears. The torment he sees in Hell is great that it leaves him sad for all mankind who choose to ignore the love of God.

Message from Archangel Israfael

Enlightenment comes from knowledge, and knowledge

comes through learning. Wisdom is the result of listening to your inner voice and following its guidance. My assignment in the Angel Peace Garden is to help you surround yourself with positive energy. Noise upheaval and inner turmoil must be overcome for you to find the stillness you seek, and then you must listen to the inner voice of spirit. You live in a beautiful world, but too often the stresses of your lives can leave you feeling bereft and in need of spiritual nourishment. When you employ a garden designer to help you create you sacred oasis, you listen carefully to their advise and despite the cost you are willing to make sacrifices to achieve your goal. So it is with accessing peace and harmony within yourself. Set aside time each day to connect with God; it is not as difficult as you imagine.

Archangel Raziel

His name means 'Secret of the Creator' and he belongs to the Celestial Choir of the Cherubim. It is said that Raziel is an angel of the secret regions and is 'Chief of the Supreme Mysteries.' (1,500 keys to the mysteries of Heaven).

He is patron of the first human, Adam, and it is said that he stands at the veil separating God from creation and records everything said at the Throne of God. He is the author of a book called the Tome from which Noah gained the information to build the Ark. Raziel is recognised by the yellow aura around him and by his large wings, which are sky blue in colour. He is the guardian of originality, pure ideas, and dreams. He is known to exceptionally helpful and supportive to those seeking clarity on any issue. Raziel understands the power, speed, and flow of electrical energy systems in the universe.

Message from Archangel Raziel

I AM Raziel and my role is to aid those who seek divine enlightenment. I am your advocate and messenger sent from God who wishes you to benefit from your time on Earth. Be still and rejoice in the stillness, we are waiting for you to join us. We are all around you working tirelessly on your behalf. My task is to protect and care for benefactors, those caregivers who give so generously of themselves to those who are in any kind of need. Benefactors come in all forms; they may be of the angelic realm, they may be a member of your family or relations and friends now in spirit. Soul seekers who have heard of your need and volunteer to help.

Archangel Raphael

His name means 'God has Healed.' He is a senior archangel who has been given responsibility for the healing of all God's peoples in the entire universe. There are many examples of Raphael's healing ministry recorded in the sacred books of the major world religions. He is one of the most loved of all the angels and is still being painted by artists today. It is said that when Solomon prayed to God for aid in building the temple in Jerusalem, Raphael personally delivered the gift of a magic ring that had the power to overcome demons.

Message from Raphael

I am the Archangel Raphael and I represent the healing power of the living God, who desires that you be free of all ills that separate you from him. I bring you love from the God who made you in his own image. I have been given the responsibility of caring for all children. When called upon, I care for and defend all children who are abused or exploited in any way. I come in love and bring the healing of a very generous God. Know that even in your darkest times, I am there with you walking beside you through it all. When you raise your heart and mind to God, angels are immediately sent to your side to comfort you. No request is ever ignored when you ask help is given.

The Archangel Ariel

His name means 'Lion of God.' He is one of the seven princes who rule the waters of the Earth. Ariel is one of the overlighting angels, and he is mentioned in several of the worlds Holy Books. He is one of the Thrones who sing the praises of God. It is said that he and Raphael have joined forces to cure disease and alleviate the suffering of all mankind.

Message from Archangel Ariel

I am the Archangel Ariel and I am present in the North Eastern area of the Angel Peace Garden. I have been given the task of helping you to raise your awareness and develop your personal relationships. I will also assist you to develop your relationship with God and your higher self. I will help you to see where your destiny lies and find the meaning and purpose to your time on Earth. Embrace God's love and experience real joy that is selfless, forgiving, and unconditional.

Archangel Gabriel

His name means 'God is my strength.' He is also known as the 'heavenly awakener' it was Gabriel who appeared to Mary at her Annunciation to tell her she would conceive and bear a son who would be the Son of God. It has also been recorded by scholars that Gabriel appeared to Mary's cousin to tell her that she too would bear a son who would be John the Baptist. Muslims believe that Gabriel is the Spirit of Troth who dictated the Koran to the prophet Mohammed. In Jewish tradition it is believed that it was Gabriel who parted the waters of the Red Sea.

Message from Archangel Gabriel

I am the Archangel of the South and I greet you in the name of our beloved God who loves all without exception. My assignment is to assist you in reaching your full potential and discover all the talents that you possess. I will act as a go-between in difficult situations. I am also the patron of global communications. I am responsible for facilitating changes in your life that will open doors for your happiness.

Archangel Metatron

His name means 'one that occupies the Throne of God.' He is seen as liberating angel who, according to history, wrestled with Jacob. He is said to hold the highest rank of all the angels. There is no reference to him in the scriptures, but nonetheless he has many titles. They are Chancellor of Heaven, King of the Angels, Highest Power of Abundance, and The Supreme Angel of Death. He is the twin brother of Sandalphon, keeper of the sacred scrolls, and is also overseer of the planet Uranus. He has lived on Earth as the prophet Enoch who was taken up to Heaven and transformed into an 'angel of fire' with thirty-six pairs of wings. Metatron is said to be the angel who stopped Abraham sacrificing his son Isaac and who led the Hebrews through the wilderness for forty years.

Message from Metatron

I am the Archangel Metatron who speaks to you in love and brings blessings from the most high Creator. I oversee the projects and bring forward whichever angels are appropriate. There are many angels who are available to help you achieve your goals and reach for enlightenment. I once lived among you and know of the difficulties and discomforts that life can bring. Life is in many ways unchanged, Man is still seeking to find himself but is frequently frustrated in his efforts. If you are experiencing despair, fear not, I am there with you. I will help you realise your dreams, all you need to do is ask and quiet yourself to hear the answer.

A Thought from the Author

Metatron is the 'hound of heaven' searching out lost souls so they can behold the face of the Creator. When we call upon him, we are never disappointed with the results. In March 2003 I was presented with a beautiful painting of the Archangel Metatron, which was painted by a lovely lady called Alison Knox. On the back was this simple message:

'Given to Sean Jude Bradley to heal souls broken by Men in ignorance and pain.'

Messages from the Archangels arrived on the 29th September 2000, which is the Feast of the Archangel Princes.

The Angel Circle

The angel circle is part of the Divine Blueprint that is central to the creation of a sacred garden. It is a celebration of the tireless efforts of the angels of the Nature Wave and the Animal Kingdom. They are the stalwarts who have supervised not only the four elements, but also the animal kingdom and the plant-life of the Earth from the beginning of time. They take their directives from God via the Archangel Princes who in turn delegate areas of responsibility to the Elementals.

It is my hope that Man will make more and more positive choices to preserve and protect the planet and work hand in hand with the angels of all the realms to repair the damage already done. One fairly recent example is the 'foot and mouth' outbreak in 2001. There was deep sadness in the realms of nature at the appalling waste of life, which was caused in the main by our carelessness. It is hoped we have learned a collective lesson and will take more care of our animal and plant kingdoms in the future.

When we take a closer look at the sacred circle, we can see that not only is it divided into four key areas representing North, South, East, and West, but that each of the four compartments has an associated colour. If we look at the outer ring of the blue compartment, we will see that it is under the Divine influence of the Archangel Michael. If we move to the next ring, we find he is the Prince of the North. Moving to the next section, we see he bring with him angel helpers and the fourth compartment tells us that the whole project is overseen by the Archangel Metatron. In the very centre, you will see a symbol that signifies the sun and the moon's rays. These are the two great energies that allow us to survive on this planet; they represent the 'Universal Life Force Energy,' which along with water sustains life.

I noticed that the associated colours of the angels in the Bagua are different from those attributed to them in some books. I questioned this and was told that the Archangel Princes were placed according to the frequency at which they resonate and the direction i.e. north, south, east, and west. Neither the others or myself are wrong, there are just different energies required for different tasks.

Angels of the Zodiac

♑

Capricorn
21st December to 19th January

NAME	ORPHIEL
MEANING	I order
ELEMENT	Earth
ARCHANGEL	Samael–Saturn
STONE	Tourmaline
GIFT	Antique box
QUALITY	Cardinal
KEYWORD	Reverence
COLOUR	Indigo
METAL	Lead
MANIFESTS	Concentration, power

♒

Aquarius
20th January to 18th February

NAME	CAMBIEL
MEANING	I empower
ELEMENT	Air
ARCHANGEL	Raziel–Uranus
STONE	Sapphire
GIFT	Sapphire Ring
QUALITY	Fixed
KEYWORD	Truth
COLOUR	Electric Blue
METAL	Aluminum
MANIFESTS	Curiosity

Pisces
19th February to 20th March

NAME	BARAKIEL
MEANING	I love
ELEMENT	Water
ARCHANGEL	Zaphkiel–Neptune
STONE	Rose Quartz
GIFT	Seashell Slippers
QUALITY	Mutable
KEYWORD	Unity
COLOUR	Rose pink
METAL	Platinum
MANIFESTS	Insight

♈

Aries
21st March to 20th April

NAMES	ARAQUIEL
MEANING	I am
ELEMENT	Fire
ARCHANGEL	Hanael–Mars
STONE	Diamond
GIFT	Crown
QUALITY	Cardinal
KEYWORD	Hope
COLOUR	Red
METAL	Iron
MANIFESTS	Energy

♉

Taurus
21st April to 20th May

NAME	ASHMODIAL
MEANING	I become
ELEMENT	Earth
ARCHANGEL	Sandalphon–Earth
STONE	Emerald
GIFT	Necklace
QUALITY	Fixed
KEYWORD	Peace
COLOUR	Green
METAL	Copper
MANIFESTS	Strength

II

Gemini
21st May to 20th June

NAME	AMBRIEL
MEANING	I circulate
ELEMENT	Air
ARCHANGEL	Gabriel–Mercury
STONE	Aquamarine
GIFT	Agate horn
QUALITY	Mutable
KEYWORD	Joy
COLOUR	Yellow
METAL	Quicksilver
MANIFESTS	Change

♋

Cancer
21st June to 21st July

NAME	CAEL
MEANING	I create
ELEMENT	Water
ARCHANGEL	Auriel–Moon
STONE	Pearl
GIFT	Breastplate
QUALITY	Cardinal
KEYWORD	Patience
COLOUR	Sea Blue
METAL	Silver
MANIFESTS	Fexibility

♌

Leo

22nd July to 21st August

NAME	ZERACHIEL
MEANING	I rule
ELEMENT	Fire
ARCHANGEL	Michael–The Sun
STONE	Ruby
GIFT	A golden shield
QUALITY	Fixed
KEYWORD	Faith
COLOUR	Orange
METAL	Gold
MANIFESTS	Understanding

♍

Virgo
22nd August to 21st September

NAME	VAEL
MEANING	I provide
ELEMENT	Earth
ARCHANGEL	Shekinah–Charon
STONE	Jasper
GIFT	A girdle
QUALITY	Mutable
KEYWORD	Purity
COLOUR	White
METAL	Platinum
MANIFESTS	Grace

Ω

Libra
22nd September to 22nd October

NAME	ZURIEL
MEANING	I soothe
ELEMENT	Air
ARCHANGEL	Raphael–Venus
STONE	Amethyst
GIFT	An Opal Scabbard
QUALITY	Cardinal
KEYWORD	Beauty
COLOUR	Lilac
METAL	Copper
MANIFESTS	Balance

♏

Scorpio
23rd October to 21st November

NAME	BARUEL
MEANING	I heal
ELEMENT	Water
ARCHANGEL	Metatron–Pluto
STONE	Topaz
GIFT	Jewelled dagger
QUALITY	Fixed
KEYWORD	Justice
COLOUR	Black
METAL	Steel
MANIFESTS	Determination

✗

Sagittarius
22nd November to 20th December

NAME	ADNACHIEL
MEANING	I encourage
ELEMENT	Fire
ARCHANGEL	Zadkiel–Jupiter
STONE	Turquoise
GIFT	A bow
QUALITY	Mutable
KEYWORD	Wisdom
COLOUR	Purple
METAL	Tin
MANIFESTS	Creativity

Angels and What They Do

ADDICTIONS
Archangel Raphael

ALCHEMY
Archangel Raziel
Archangel Uriel

FINDING LOST PETS
Archangel Raphael
Angels of Nature and animal kingdom

HEALING
Archangel Raphael
Healing Angels.

ANSWERED PRAYERS
Archangel Sandalphon

RESOLVING ARGUMENTS
Archangel Raguel

ARTISTS
Archangel Gabriel
Archangel Jophiel

AUTHORITY FIGURES
Saint Michael

BEAUTIFUL THOUGHTS
Archangel Jophiel

BENEFACTORS
Archangel Raziel

CAREER
Archangel Chamuel
Archangel Michael

CELEBRATION
Archangel Metatron

CEREMONIES
Archangel Israfael

CHAKRA CLEARING
Archangel Michael

CHI ENERGY
Archangel Israfael

CHILDREN
Archangel Gabriel
Archangel Raphael
Archangel Metatron.

CONCEPTION AND FERTILITY
Archangel Gabriel
Archangel Uriel

CRYSTAL CHILDREN
Archangel Metatron

DETERMING SEX OF UNBORN BABY
Archangel Sandalphon

HEALING
Archangel Raphael

INDIGO CHILDREN
Archangel Metatron

PROTECTION
Archangel Michael

INCREASING CLAIRVOYANCE
Archangel Raphael
Archangel Jeremiel
Archangel Haniel
Archangel Raziel

COMPASSION
Archangel Zadkiel

COOPERATION FROM OLDER PEOPLE
Archangel Raguel

COURAGE
Archangel Michael

ELIMINATING OR REDUCING CRAVINGS
Archangel Raphael

DETOXIFICATION
Archangel Raphael

DIRECTION LIFE PURPOSE
Archangel Michael.

DIVINE MAGIC
Archangel Ariel
Archangel Raziel

DREAMS
Archangel Jeremiel

EARTH CHANGES
Archangel Uriel

EMPOWERMENT
Archangel Raguel

ENERGY
Archangel Michael

ENERGY–THE ENVIRONMENT
. Archangel Ariel

THE ESOTERIC
Archangel Raziel

EYESIGHT
Archangel Raphael

FAME
Archangel Gabriel

FAITH ISSUES
Archangel Raphael

FAMILY
Archangel Uriel

FORGIVENESS
Archangel Zadkiel
GRACE
Archangel Haniel

GRIEVING
Archangel Azrael

HARMONY IN FAMILIES
Archangel Raguel

GENERAL HARMONY
Archangel Uriel

HARMONY FOR GROUPS
Archangel Raguel

HARMONY WHILE TRAVELLING AWAY FROM
HOME
Archangel Raphael

HEALERS
Archangel Raphael
Healing Angels

HEALING ANIMALS
Archangel Raphael
Archangel Ariel
Archangel Raziel

HEALING ALL EYE AILMENTS
Archangel Raphael.

CHANCELLOR OF HEAVEN
Archangel Metatron

HOME / SPACE CLEARING
Archangel Michael
Archangel Raphael

INTERIOR DESIGN AND DECORATING
Archangel Jophiel

JOURNALISM
Archangel Gabriel
Archangel Ariel

KNOWLEDGE
Archangel Ariel
Archangel Uriel

LABYRINTHS
Archangel Raziel

LIFE PURPOSE
Archangel Chamuel
Archangel Michael

LOVE
Archangel Camael

LOST PROPERTY
Archangel Chamuel
Archangel Zadkiel

MANIFESTING
Archangels Ariel and Raziel

MECHANICAL PROBLEMS
Archangel Michael
Archangel Ariel

MEMORY ENHANCEMENT
Archangel Zadkiel
Archangel Ariel

MERCY
Archangel Gabriel

MOON ENERGY
Archangel Haniel

MOTIVATION
Archangel Michael

MUSIC
Archangel Gabriel
Archangel Sandalphon

ORGANISATIONS
Archangel Metatron
Archangel Raguel

PATIENCE
Archangel Michael

PEACE
Archangel Chamuel

PROCRASTINATION
Archangel Michael

PROPHETIC ABILITIES
Archangel Jeremiel

PROTECTION OF THE OCEANS
Archangel Ariel

PROTECTION OF TRAVELERS
Archangel Raphael

RECORD KEEPING
Archangel Metatron

INCREASE SELF-ESTEEM
Archangel Michael

SALVATION
Archangel Uriel

UNDERSTANDING SPIRITUALITY ISSUES
Archangel Metatron
Archangel Uriel

STUDENTS AND STUDYING
Archangel Uriel
Archangel Zadkiel

TEMPERANCE
Archangel Cassiel

VITALITY
Archangel Michael

WEIGHT LOSS
Archangel Raphael

WRITERS AND WRITING PROJECTS
Archangel Gabriel
Archangel Uriel
Archangel Metatron

Angelic Involvement in Biblical Times

ANGELS ADVISE	Matthew 1:18-23
ANGELS ANNOUNCE MESSAGES	Matthew 2:13
ANGELS ASCEND AND DESCEND	Genesis 28: 12;
	John 1
ANGELS COMFORT	Acts 27:23-24.
ANGELS COMMUNICATE	Zechariah 1:9;
	Luke 1:34-35
ANGELS GIVE DIRECTION	Acts 8: 26.
ANGELS FEED	1 Kings: 19: 5-7
ANGELS FIGHT OUR BATTLES	Exodus 33: 2
ANGELS FIND THE LOST	Genesis 16: 7
ANGELS GUARD	Psalm 34: 7
ANGELS HEAL	Job 33: 20-24
ANGELS MINISTER TO CHRIST	Matthew 4: 11;
	Mark 1: 1
ANGELS MINISTER TO PEOPLE	Hebrews 1:14
ANGELS PRAISE GOD	Luke 2: 13-14
ANGELS PREACH	Galatians 1: 8
ANGELS PROCLAIM	Revelation 5: 2
ANGELS PROTEST	Zechariah 3: 4
ANGELS PROVIDE	1 Kings 19: 5-7
ANGELS SAVE FROM DEATH	Daniel 6: 22
ANGELS SET FREE	Acts 5: 19;
	12: 7-9
ANGELS SPEAK THE TRUTH	Hebrews 2: 2
ANGELS WARN	Matthew 2: 13
ANGELS WORSHIP	Isaiah 6:2
	Revelation 5: 11-12

CHAKRAS

CHAKRAS

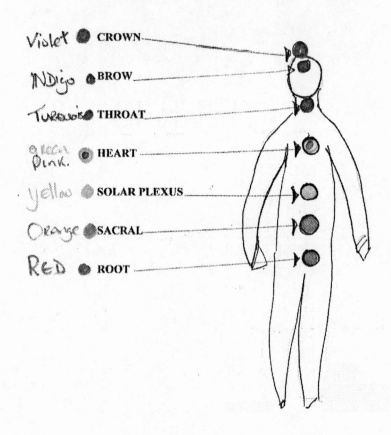

Violet ● CROWN

NDigo ● BROW

Turavise ● THROAT

green
Pink. ● HEART

yellow ● SOLAR PLEXUS

Orange ● SACRAL

Red ● ROOT

Chakras

The word chakra is from the Sanskrit word which means wheel. The body has seven major and twenty-one minor ones. They are spinning vortices of energy, which when in balance promote a feeling of health and well-being. Each one has an associated colour, issue, body part, etc. If the chakra is out of balance we can experience symptoms in our physical bodies. For more information on this see the books listed in the bibliography. I have listed some of the associations for each one, but as I am not an expert on charkas I have kept the list quite general.

FIRST CHAKRA – ROOT

Sanskrit name	Muladhara
Meaning	Root or Support
Colour	Red
Issue	Survival
Gland	Adrenals
Body part	Skeleton, bones
Sense	Smell
Musical note	C
Crystal	Bloodstone, hematite
Developmental age	1 to 8
Lesson	Standing up for self

SECOND CHAKRA – SACRAL

Sanskrit name	Svadhisthana
Meaning	Sweetness
Colour	Orange
Issue	Emotional balance/sexuality
Gland	Ovaries/Testes
Body part	Sex organs/bladder/womb
Sense	Taste
Musical note	D
Crystal	Citrine
Developmental age	8 to 14
Lesson	Motivation

THIRD CHAKRA – SOLAR PLEXUS

Sanskrit name	Manipura
Meaning	Lustrous Gem
Colour	Yellow
Issue	Will/power
Gland	Pancreas
Body part	Digestive system/muscles
Sense	Sight
Musical note	E
Crystal	Aventurine/quartz
Developmental age	14 to 21 years
Lesson	self-esteem/confidence

FOURTH CHAKRA – HEART

Sanskrit name	Anahata
Meaning	Unstruck
Colour	Green/pink
Issue	Love and relationships
Gland	Thymus
Body part	Heart/chest/lungs
Sense	Touch
Musical note	F
Crystal	Emerald/tourmaline
Developmental age	21 to 28 years
Lesson	Forgiveness/compassion

FIFTH CHAKRA – THROAT

Sanskrit name	Vishuddha
Meaning	Purification
Colour	Blue
Issue	Communication
Gland	Thyroid
Body part	Mouth/throat/ears
Sense	Sound/hearing
Musical note	G
Crystal	Turquoise/lapis lazuli
Developmental age	28 to 35 years
Lesson	Personal expression

SIXTH CHAKRA – THIRD EYE

Sanskrit name	Ajna
Meaning	To know
Colour	Indigo
Issue	Wisdom/intuition
Gland	Pituitary
Body part	Eyes/base of skull
Sense	Sixth sense
Musical note	A
Crystal	Amethyst/fluorite
Developmental age	N/A
Lesson	Emotional intelligence

SEVENTH CHAKRA – CROWN

Sanskrit name	Sahasrara
Meaning	Thousandfold
Colour	Violet
Issue	Spirituality
Gland	Pineal
Body part	Skull/brain/skin
Sense	Beyond self
Musical note	B
Crystal	Amethyst/clear quartz
Development age	N/A
Lesson	Selflessness

21 SECONDARY / MINOR CHAKRAS

EARS ————

CHEEKS ————
(NOT EYES)

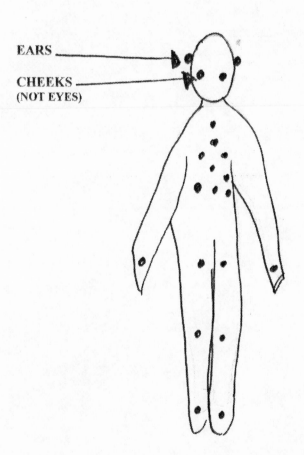

THE AURA

AURA

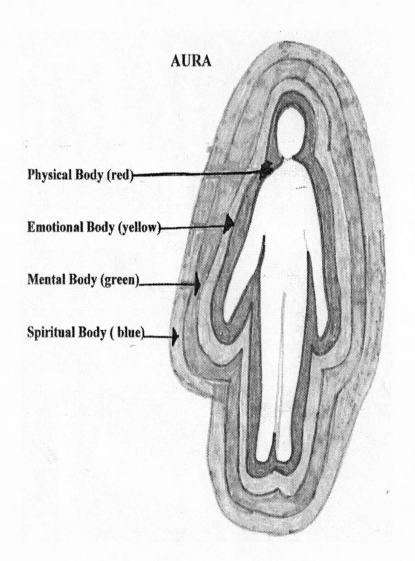

Physical Body (red)

Emotional Body (yellow)

Mental Body (green)

Spiritual Body (blue)

The Aura

AURA

The human aura is made up of several 'layers' called energy bodies. They vibrate at different frequencies and have different associated colours. Each body surrounds and intermingles with all the lower ones including the physical body. (i.e. the emotional body 'mingles' with the etheric and physical bodies.)

PHYSICAL

We are all familiar with our physical bodies. They contain our organs, cells, tissues, etc. It is the densest of all the bodies as it vibrates at a low frequency.

ETHERIC

The etheric holds the 'blueprint' for the physical body. Anything in the etheric body will eventually be reflected in the physical. Some healers and clairvoyants can see illness in the etheric before it manifests in the physical.

EMOTIONAL

The emotional body holds the patterns, which are formed, by beliefs from the mental body. This layer is also known as the astral body.

MENTAL

Here we store our cultural beliefs, our belief in ourselves, and who we are as people.

SPIRITUAL

Holds our higher purpose, intentions, and our goals. This holds our sense of connection to the world and other people. Our conscience and our connection to Source/God /Universe.

The Energy Angels

Be still and quiet, my child, now, for I have a story to
tell.
About the Angels and their energy that swirls around
and smells.
It smells of roses and lavender and shimmers like new
fallen snow.
It is all around you night and day and this is what you
must know.

For all God's creatures have colour and the shades have
meaning as well.
From ruby red to apple green and maybe purple around
your head.
Archangel Michael is sapphire blue with his sword in his
hand.
While Archangel Raphael's is emerald green the colour
of our land.

There are Angels for the seasons, the months, and each
day.
For morning and for evening time with those who sing
and pray.
Even when you skip and jump, there's an Angel by your
side.
To help you take the next big step as your constant loving
guide.

The Angels of Nature are special and want to be children's
friends.
For God beams their energy to this world in coloured
lights to mend

The damage done to Mother Earth by humans through
all time.
So let us begin and feel their love and get this world to
shine!

Call upon the angels when you are sad and feeling low.
Imagine a golden bubble in which you sit, shine, and
glow!
Breathe in this shiny golden light through every part of
you.
Then when you open up your eyes you will know just
what to do!

So, children, next time you see a rainbow, make sure to
stop and stare
At the many different colours and the energy that is there.
For the Angels have been busy making all these colours
shine,
Breathe in their love and cherish it as it really is divine!

By Grainne Tyndall of Angels at Play.
April 2004

GARDENS

A Seed is Planted

Being someone who lives with being Bi Polar, I have learned over the years to fight the 'blues.' When I felt down, I would spend hours working in the garden. I felt safe there; it was energising, healing, and tranquil. I also noticed that surrounding myself with certain colours would have a positive impact on my moods. I also found that some smells improved my sense of well-being. The plants themselves were very soothing to be around.

Some years ago, when I lived in Manchester, my partner and I bought a special dwarf standard tree. It was very beautiful and elegant with its profusion of white daisy-like flowers. One afternoon a storm blew it down and its stem snapped into two pieces. My horticultural experience told me to bin the plant as once the stem is severed it can't be repaired or saved. Once again instinct took over and I decided to have a go at saving the tree. I joined the two pieces of the stem together as closely and tightly as I could with strong tape and then used three medium sized bamboo canes to make splints. Then I gave the plant healing for a full fifteen minutes. I invoked the Angels of Nature to continue with the healing and support the plant. The plant flourished; the same healing that worked with animals, worked with plants too. From here on in the feeling that I was to begin doing healing work with people became stronger and stronger.

Ground Rules for the Angel Peace Garden

If we are one with nature and ourselves then we will know that we are in the presence of the Divine in our sacred oasis. Our sacred oasis can be our garden, home, or that place of stillness inside ourselves that we retreat to in those times when we need some peace. It is important that we behave appropriately so that the peace and integrity of the space is protected. There you can be alone with God and celebrate your life. Honour nature's gifts that are yours to cherish and enjoy. You don't have to be a brilliant designer or spend a fortune to be able to create a beautiful space that you can enjoy; all you need is willingness and a love of nature.

The Healing Energy of Trees

I only have to walk through a forest to experience sheer delight and feelings of absolute joy and peace. The pure air and the sounds emanating from the forest creates a deep feeling of inner bliss.

There is a wise old saying that says, " You are near to God in your Garden."

Trees have an important part to play in our healing process. Throughout the centuries, mankind has had a strong relationship with tree energies and benefited greatly from them.

According to Flower A Newhouse, when you see a Tree Diva it is an unforgettable experience and one that leaves a lasting impression on your mind, body, and in your spirit.

Being in the presence of a tree deva is a wonderful experience that usually results in one wanting to go up to the tree and hug it. Whenever I feel tired and weary, I stand in front of my favourite tree and just embrace its energy and invite its healing to saturate my being.

I often stand with my back to my favourite tree and invite the healing energies of Mother Earth to flow up through my feet and right through my body. This ritual is both meditative and healing. As well as balancing my Chakras, it leaves me fully grounded and gives me a deep sense of peace.

Trees have an uncanny way of drawing us to them. They ask that we respect their energy and in return they share their vibrational healing energies with us.

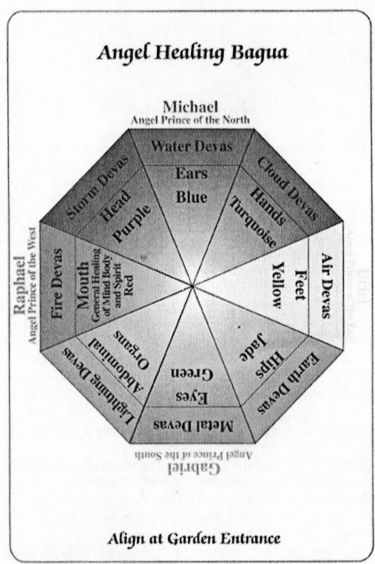

Angel Healing Bagua

Michael
Angel Prince of the North

Water Devas
Storm Devas
Cloud Devas
Ears
Blue
Head
Purple
Hands
Turquoise
Raphael
Angel Prince of the West
Fire Devas
Mouth
General Healing of Mind Body and Spirit
Red
Air Devas
Feet
Yellow
Abdominal Organs
Lightning Devas
Eyes
Green
Jade
Hips
Earth Devas
Metal Devas
Gabriel
Angel Prince of the South

Align at Garden Entrance

www.angelgardens4u.com

Sacred Angel Circle

North West

North East

Arch Angel Michael
Angel Prince of the North
Colour Blue

Angel Helpers

Arch Angel Uriel
Angel Prince of the East
Colour Yellow

Angel Helpers

Metatron

Arch Angel Raphael
Angel Prince of the West
Colour Red

Angel Helpers

Angel Helpers

Arch Angel Gabriel
Angel Prince of the South
Colour Green

South West

South East

Align at Garden Entrance

The Symbolic Meanings of Flowers

Flower Meaning

Flower	Meaning
Violet	Virtue and faithfulness
Aster and Myrtle	Love
Pansy	Happiness
Magnolia	Dignity
Lilly of the Valley	Humility
Bluebell and Holly	Humility
Heather	Admiration
White Lilly	Purity
Yellow Lilly	Truthfulness
Freesia	Faith
Crocus	Cheerfulness
Amaryllis	Pride
Anemone	Sincerity
Chrysanthemum	Truth
Forsythia	Expectation
Lilac	Beauty

Sacred Plants and Theirs Meanings

Aspidistra	Fortitude
Chrysanthemum	Resolution
Cypress	Nobility
Gardenia	Strength
Hydrangea	Achievement
Kerria	Individualism
Orchid	Endurance
Peony	Wealth
Pine	Longevity
Pomegranate	Fertility
Rhododendron	Delicacy
Virginia Creeper	Tenacity

Yin and Yang Energy Plants

Nowhere is the duality of the opposing yet complementary forces of Yin and Yang more pronounced than in an angel sacred peace garden.

YIN (Negative) Plants	YANG (Positive) Plants
Apricot	Bamboo
Jasmine	Cherry
Magnolia	Chrysanthemum
Pear	Orchids
Rhododendron	Peony
Rose	Willow

Testimonial

I received this testimonial from a lovely lady in Scotland. She came to me for a one to one treatment and then went on to do the Therapist's Course. I wish to thank her for allowing me to include it in this book.

I had never heard of Therapeutic Touch or Channelling until a friend told me about Sean's work as a healer and channeller using angelic love and light. The course has transformed my life to the point where I can breathe, let go, and let my Goddess be. For years I was trapped by memories of sexual abuse, and through doing the course I was empowered to look at my wounded child with and be set free! The last day of the course also helped me to reclaim my inner being and permit myself to experience real joy and laughter again after 48 years of living in 'hell.' I was overwhelmed to meet my beautiful Archangel Metatron. At first I called him Ministroni, but he knew what I meant.

Aggie – Scotland.

For those who wish to study and deepen their knowledge, Sean has developed some accredited courses. Here is a little of the feedback he has received about them.

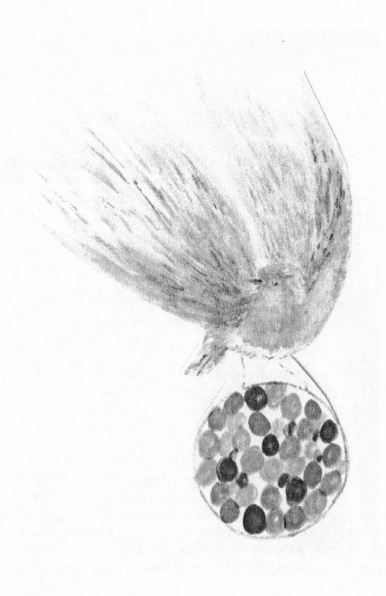

The Three-Day Therapists Course

This course is aimed at those who are already working with healing energy in some form or another. Students who complete the course receive a certificate in Therapeutic Channelling.

Working long hours as a therapist prevented me from getting into a support group. Having completed the course in Ireland in August 2003, I am delighted to be a part of a family of therapists. When I hit rock bottom, they are there to help me cope. We meet up fortnightly and share the joys as well as the sorrows! Thanks everyone.

Angie BK – Wicklow.

I enjoyed the advanced three-day course for practitioners as it empowered me to develop an ancient skill that has been in circulation for centuries.

J Tulle – N. I.

Up until very recently, I was giving to the point of denying myself! The course in Therapeutic Channelling has empowered me to be more selfish in a strange sort of way. I have been made aware that I have specific needs as a human being and as a therapist caring for others. I have been warmly accepted as a valued member of the team and enjoy being a part of a loving group who know how to care for each other.

Jo S – Midlands.

The Six-Day Course for Beginners

This course is also for students who wish to become practitioners of Therapeutic Channelling. Students receive a certificate when they have completed the their probationary period of training at the end of the course.

The course was unlike any other I have been to. The energies were perfect and the group was ordinary people searching for a meaning and a purpose to their lives and looking for a new way of connecting with their clients. Sean taught us to combine humour and laughter and helped us develop a sense of the divine energies and the sacred influences in our work as potential channellers. I learned practical skills that have enhanced my work with my clients and students. The group was very supportive.

Trisha – Notts.

It is refreshing to be a part of something as vibrant and healing as Therapeutic Pathways consultancy. The six-day course touched a lot of painful memories that needed to be healed so that I could move forward. "Physician heal thyself" will forever remain with me from my time on the course. How true it was then and more importantly now! We cannot touch another's life till we have healed and restored ourselves.

Jenny T – Cambridge UK.

For full details of all courses e-mail Sean at seansacademy@aol.com or visit his website www.sean-bradley.com

Sean's Retreat Centre
Chapel Gap

Our aim is to provide peace and respite for those in caring roles that just need a little bit of rest and relaxation. One to one sessions with Sean are also available depending on Sean's commitments. We aim to tailor each stay to the individual's needs.

For further information, dates and costs please telephone No: +0044-1524-762292
or e-mail seansacadeny@aol.com—www.sean-bradley.com

Preparing Yourself for 2012

ANNOUNCE
1-DAY CONFERENCE
LET YOUR DIVINE LIGHT SHINE!

"A Day working with the Christ /Angelic Healing
Energies /underpinned by the Philosophy of the Essenes."

We will open your hearts and souls to the Christ
Consciousness in the presence of Angels, that you may be
empowered to self heal all that is broken, wounded and in
pain.

With
Sean Bradley Consultant, Healer and Life Coach
& Therapists of the Sean Bradley Academy
(UK & Ireland)
Author of *Angelic Energies / Create An Oasis for Angels*
(release due 2005)

Registration & Coffee 9.15am
Conference Starts at 10 AM TO 4 PM

Fee: A moderate price to be announced

LIMITED PLACES APPLY!
Vegetarian Buffet style Lunch & Refreshments included in price.

Details from: Sean Bradley Academy of Therapeutic
Channelling for Practitioners
www.sean-bradley.com

2005 TOUR
1-Day Conference

2005	**Let Your Light Shine**
1 May 2005	Derbyshire
9 July 2005	Dublin, Ireland
13 August '05	London
27 August '05	Newcastle
10 September	Glasgow, Scotland
26 September	Sheffield
2 October '05	Manchester
15 October '05	Cardiff South Wales
22 October '05	Southport, Merseyside UK
12 November '05	Harrogate, Yorkshire
11 December'05	Cork City, Ireland

BRINGING OUR TOUR TO YOU

If you would like to host this beautiful 1-Day Conference, then please e-mail or write to the Academy for details. We are now taking bookings for 2006.

Embracing Christ Consciousness through the Heart Chakra

Centuries ago, the Essenes, living in the Middle East, were given a set of divine rules that would help them to walk the path of faith and experience the bountiful blessing from their God.

Today, you and I are invited to embrace the divine essence of God in Jesus Christ. Jesus invites us to embrace the Christ consciousness in love. If we are willing to walk this spiritual path with Jesus Christ, then we believe and accept that it will lead us to our God. In our acceptance we embrace the Christ consciousness as a new way of life. Living in the Christ Consciousness we are invited to adopt specific core values that will empower us to self heal and reclaim our dignity as sons and daughters of God. Love represents loving God in yourself, your neighbour, and everything or anything that lives, moves, and has their being from God. The Light represents the presence of the divine in all–in you and me–the landscapes–the elements–the animal kingdom–the seasons. Love and Light unites the God in us–in you and in me. Love and Light is Christ Consciousness.

When we say to our friends or sign our correspondence with Love and Light we are in fact making a positive statement. We are saying that Christ consciousness is alive–well and kicking! When we embrace Love and Light we are showering divine blessedness throughout the universe. Connecting with our heart centre is essential as it releases the important spiritual triggers that infuse us with clarity of perception and integrity of spirit.

When we embrace the divine love and light of Christ consciousness, we are empowered to connect with our own inner child through our heart centre. If we discover that in our wounded-ness we are trapped, then we can release everything to the divine light of God. When we transmute through our high heart chakra, all negative energies associated with deep-rooted pain, shame, non-forgiveness, resentment, harboured grudges, lack of self-respect we become infused with Love and Compassion.

Our ascension is a step-by-step process of releasing, clearing, and cleansing our emotional blockages layer by layer. As each layer is removed, we attain a higher level of understanding of the divine mystery of Christ consciousness and our individual DNA is re-coded empowering us to transcend to a higher vibrational energy. Love and compassion are the keys that facilitate this process and the more we let go and permit God to be in our Minds-in our bodies and in our dealings with self–with others, our higher self accelerates and ascends. The Messengers of God empower us in our Ascension /Healing process!

> When we connect with our heart centre we touch the very fibres of our being. As a child of the light–a child of God, we embrace the Divine within us. Our heart centre is the consciousness of Christ in God. The Christ consciousness empowers us to look at yourself

through the eyes of unconditional selfless healing love. When we engage with our own divinity there is an immediate rising of our spiritual awareness that we are one with God and God is one with us.

In the presence of this absolute, unconditional healing love and light of Christ, we are empowered to take back our control and personal power.

Sean's next book, *Connecting with the Christ /Angelic Energies* will hopefully be available for publication autumn of 2005.

1-DAY CONFERENCE PROGRAMME
LET YOUR DIVINE LIGHT SHINE

10:00AM   Welcome Address by David Cox
Crystal Clear Promotions.

Overview of the day.

WORKSHOP 1: What is Christ Consciousness?

11:00am   Coffee Break

11:20   A healing meditation
Connecting with the Sacred Heart Chakra /
Christ.

11:50   Comfort break (5 mins) Quiet Music

11:55   Workshop 2: Sacred Tools –Religion and
Spirituality
Preparing you for 2012
12:30   Lunch Break

2pm: Welcome Back

2:10pm   Workshop 3: The Philosophy of the Essenes
(Founding Fathers of Angelology).

2:40pm   Comfort break. (5 mins). Quiet Music

2:45pm   Workshop 4 : Channelling Divine Love
through 'Healing Touch.' Working in
partnership with Angelic energy.

3:13pm   Coffee Break. Quiet Music

3:30pm   Concluding Healing Meditation
          "Angel Visualization of Therapeutic Touch."
4pm   Farewell Sing a long.

The Sean Bradley Academy of Therapeutic Channelling for Practitioners

www.sean-bradley.com

Our Commitment is to work from a place of absolute integrity, empowering our clients and students to work with Sacred healing Energies incorporating the Christ Consciousness, the essence of Mary of Magdala and the Archangels and healing angels of the Celestial Bagua (Divine Blueprint given to Sean in 1998.).

The Academy offers a range of Residential and Non Residential Courses both in the UK and Abroad subject to availability. They are, as follows:

- ⊙ 5 Modular (6 day) course for Beginners in all aspects of Therapeutic Channelling /Healing. (Res/non-res).
- ⊙ 4 day Advanced Course for qualified Practitioners / Healers /Therapists. (Res /Non-Residential).
- ⊙ 3 day Residential Course in Teaching & Practice for our Therapists wishing to train Students accessing Beginner's Channelling Course / Angel healing Day.
- ⊙ 4 day (5 nights) Residential Masters Cert. Course For Practitioners.
- ⊙ Angel Empowerment Retreats (1 week) Residential. UK & Ireland.

Sean has recorded a series of recordings empowering you to experience the presence of Angels–The Christ energies–your inner wounded Child using a choice of channelled meditations to sacred music.

The Academy has also produced a series of teaching materials in CD Rom, Video, and DVD as well as the DIY Create Your Angel peace Garden set.

1 to 1 Professional Services:

- ⊙ Therapeutic Channelling Therapies.
- ⊙ Spiritual Life Coaching/Pastoral Counselling.
- ⊙ Counselling /Counselling Supervision.
- ⊙ Respite /Holidays at Secret Oasis in Storth, South Cumbria.

For further details please contact the Academy at the above web address.

Useful Contacts

TERRA SANTA
Make excellent quality organic incense. They also make aromatherapy and herbal products. Also traditional herbal medicine.
www.terrasanta.com
Telephone - 0044 (0) 161 775 9943

ALISON KNOX – Everyday Angels.
Alison does Angel paintings and did the picture of Metatron on the front cover of this book. She also does postcards and healing scarves in very beautiful colours.

Telephone - 0044 (0) 115 962 3877
Fax 0044 (0) 115 985 6878

HAZEL HUNT – Artist
Hazel painted the robin and Tree used in this book. Any enquiries about Hazel or her work, please contact her via Sean at seansacademy@aol.com

Other Title by Sean Bradley

Produced and Published by PublishAmerica.com

Create An Oasis for Angels – due out Spring 2005

Through Trauma We Are Reborn (Sean's life story overcoming mental illness)–due out summer 2005

E-Books that can be downloaded from the Internet

Angels Here I Am

A Sacred Oasis for Angels

Sacred Planting Designs For An Angel Peace Garden

Sacred Tools For Angel & Divine Connectedness

4 Seasons Healing Meditations

Therapeutic Channelling – Case Studies for Therapists.

Recordings by Luf Luf Productions
for
Sean Bradley (The Barefoot Angel Man)
Therapeutic Pathways Consultancy

Includes Post & Packaging UK

No	Title	Cost
1	*Create An Angel Peace Garden* CD	**£45.99**
2	*Come and Explore the Wonder of Angels Series* (Teaching Series about Angelic Involvement and Ministry for Beginners to Intermediate Level) **Double CD**	**£35.99**
3	*Embracing Your Inner Essence* (Practitioner Heal Thyself)	**£29.99**

7 Healing meditations empowering you to reclaim Fear & Relax in the presence of selfless love and light
Tract 1-3 ; 6-7: A Series of 5 exercises to release Fear.
Tract 4: *A Paradise Lost now Found*
Tract 5: *The Inner Child*
Tract 6: *Techniques for releasing fear.*
Tract 7: *Erasing Stress.*

4   *Your Wounded Child is your Teacher*   **£14.99**
        Tract 1:Introduction to working
              with your Inner Child.
        Tract 2: A healing Release
              meditation in the presence of
              Angels and the Christ
              Energies.

5   *Communicating with angels*   **£14.99**
        1.   Reflections
        2.   Angels empower us to take
              back control and release
              our fears.
        3.   Meet your personal angel
              meditation.

6   *Heal Yourself with the Christ Energy.*   **£14.99**
        Tract 1: Connecting you with
              the Christ Energies- a little
              light on 21.12.2012 –
        Tract 2: A healing meditation
              with Jesus Christ with your
              Heart Chakra.

7   *Angel Healing Day Collection* (**CD 9**)   **£12.99**
        Souvenir of Angel Healing Day Workshop

        Tract 1: *Meeting your Companion
              Guardian Angel* (51 mins)
        Tract 2: *A Visualization of Therapeutic
              Touch from your Guardian Angel*
              (35 mins)

8   *Angel Healing Series*   £ 19.99
4 healing meditations
Double CD
1. *Meet your personal angel*
2. *Angel visualization of*
   Channelled treatment.
3. *Release your inner child to*
   the Christ energies.
4. *Healing meditation with*
   Jesus Christ & the heart
   Chakra

9   *Heal Yourself With Angelic Love & Light*   £14.99

"Experience the powerful Christ healing energies being channelled through sacred touch. Concludes with a healing meditation and a visualization of your personal angel anointing your feet in the presence of the Archangel princes.
Tract 1: *Touched by Angels.*
Tract 2: *Angel visualization of*
channelled treatment

10   *Therapeutic Channelling Using Touch*   £15.99
(1 hour Video)
How angelic energies Channel Divine Love
    to us.
How angels touch us (feed back from
    student) Sue Presley TCCP
Angel meditation (CD 9)

11	*Relaxation Series* **Relaxation –Healing-** **Confidence Connecting with** **Nature's Gifting.** Therapeutic Pathways (Video and CD Rom)	£15.99
12	*Walking with Angels* CD Rom and Video	£15.99
13	*Festival of Angels Souvenir Video* Manchester 26th September 2004	£12.99

Distribution & Enquiries:

Crystal Clear Productions
Tel: 01254- 607610 / 07815 959548
and via website
www.sean-bradley.com

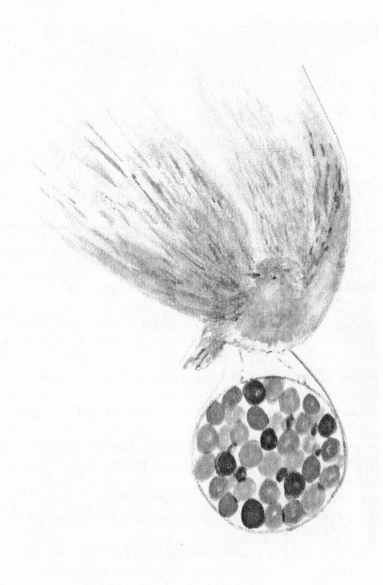

Bibliography

Anderson Joan Western, *Where Angels Walk* (Ballantine Books)

Bachelor Mary, *Prayer Collection* (Lion Publishing)

Batie Howard F, *Heal Mind, Body and Spirit* (llewellwyn 2003)

Bays Brandon, *The Journey* (Thorsons)

Brennan Barbara Ann, *Hands of Light* (Bantam New Age 1987)

Bradford Michael, *Hands on Spiritual Healing* (Findhorn Press 1994)

Buckley Michael, *His Healing Touch* (Collins Fount Paperbacks)

Burrows Ruth, *Living Love* (Darton, Longman and Todd)

Cassidy Sheila, *Sharing the Darkness* (Darton, Longman and Todd)

Cliffe Albert E, *Let Go And Let God* (Guernsey Press)

Cooper Diana, *Angel Inspiration* (Hodder & Stoughton 2001)

Cooper Diana, *A Little Light on Ascension* (Findhorn Press 1997)

Cortens Theolyn, *Living With Angels* (Piatkus 2003)

Daniel Alma, Timothy Wyllie & Andrew Ramer, *Ask Your Angels* (Piatkus 1992)

Eckersley Glennyce S, *An Angel at my Shoulder* (Rider)

Hamilton Elizabeth, *The Voice of Spirit* (Darton, Longman and Todd)

Huffines La Una, *Healing Yourself With Light* (H J Kramer Inc 1995)

Kelsey Morton, *What is Heaven Like* (New City Press)

Maddock Olivea Dewhurst, *The Book of Sound Therapy* (Gaia Books Ltd 1993)
McCarthy Flor S.D.B. *Let The Light Shine* (Kairos Publications)
McGerr Angela, *A Harmony of Angels* (Quadrille Publishing)
Muggeridge Maolcom, *Something Beautiful for God* (Fontana Books)
Newhouse Flower A, *Angels of Nature* (Quest books 1994)
O'Donohue John, *Eternal Echoes* (Bantham Books)
O'Donohoe John, *Anam Cara* (Bantam Press)
Parente Fr. Pascal P, *The Angels* (Tan Books)
Pearl Dr Eric, *The Reconnection* (Hayhouse 2004)
Peck M Scott, *The Road Less Travelled* (Arrow Books Limited)
Quest Penelope, *Reiki for Life* (Piatkus 2002)
Roland Paul, *Angels* (Piatkus)
Russell A J, *God at Eventide* (John Lunt Publishing)
Simpson Liz, *The Book of Chakra Healing* (Gaia Books Ltd 1998)
Smith Delia, *A Journey into God* (Hoddar & Stoughton)
Stevenson Sandy, *The Awakener* (Gateway 1997)
Virtue Doreen, *Healing with the Angels* (Hay House 1999)
Virtue Doreen, *Archangels & Ascended Masters* (Hay House 2003)
Virtue Doreen, *Messages from your Angels* (Hay House 2002)
Watson David, *My God is Real* (Kingsway Publications)
White Ruth, *Working with Guides & Angels* (Piatkus 1996)
White Ruth, *Working with your Chakras* (Piatkus 1997)
Woodward James, *Embracing the Chaos* (SPCK)

Printed in the United Kingdom
by Lightning Source UK Ltd.
103467UKS00002B/79-609